Philosophical Issues in Counseling and Psychotherapy

Philosophical Issues in Counseling and Psychotherapy

Encounters with Four Questions about Knowing, Effectiveness, and Truth

James T. Hansen, PhD

ROWMAN & LITTLEFIELD
Lanham • Boulder • New York • Toronto • Plymouth, UK

Published by Rowman & Littlefield
4501 Forbes Boulevard, Suite 200, Lanham, Maryland 20706
www.rowman.com

10 Thornbury Road, Plymouth PL6 7PP, United Kingdom

British Library Cataloguing in Publication Information Available

Library of Congress Cataloging-in-Publication Data

Library of Congress Cataloging-in-Publication Data Available

ISBN 978-1-4422-2877-1 (cloth : alk. paper) — ISBN 978-1-4422-2878-8 (electronic)

♾️™ The paper used in this publication meets the minimum requirements of American National Standard for Information Sciences Permanence of Paper for Printed Library Materials, ANSI/NISO Z39.48-1992.

Printed in the United States of America

To my parents, Bill and Gail, my wonderful wife Mary,
and my two extraordinary sons, Hayden and Hunter.
Thank you for all of your love and support.

Contents

Preface

I have always admired writers who share their thoughts, feelings, and struggles about their clinical work (e.g., Kottler, 2010). To help others, one has to enter into a relational matrix, full of lush meaning systems, disconcerting emotional realities, and agonizing conflicts, which are woven throughout the fabric of every life. Professional helping is inherently relational. To describe it in removed, technical language does the enterprise a disservice.

I believe that this relational principle also applies to ideas. Concepts, theories, and philosophies can be rich sources of connection, renewal, fascination, and disappointment for those who regularly court them. Indeed, these experiences may be particularly engendered by ideas from the helping professions; theories of counseling are born out of a desire to alleviate the suffering of others. Relationality, then, is in the DNA of the concepts that drive clinical work. When these concepts become rooted in intellectual soil, their relational essence can sprout, flourish, and take on a life of its own in the minds of those who contemplate them.

Ideas have always been my regular companions. They have been close partners in my struggle to resolve the intellectual conflicts that have haunted me. Courtship, idealization, fights, break-ups, reconciliations, and settling into an academic career together have all been part of my rich relational history with ideas. Thinking of concepts as something one can have a relationship with, then, is an important theme of this book.

In this regard, I have always found it ironic that descriptions of clinical work can be very engaging, while books about ideas are often dry, technical, and lifeless. If ideas are fundamentally relational, like counseling, then there is no reason that this should be the case. I wrote this book as a philosophical analogue to books that are written about clinical cases, wherein authors bring their work to life by disclosing the personal and relational elements that animate the helping process.

Before discussing the philosophical issues, I begin with a critical review of the history and current state of mental health culture. It is useful to provide an initial cultural frame to contextualize the ideas that are subsequently discussed. In the chapter that introduces the philosophical topics, I overview various justifications for philosophical inquiry in the helping professions. The heart of the book is four philosophical questions: (1) What does it mean to know a client? (2) What makes counseling effective? (3) Are truths discovered or created in the counseling relationship? (4) Should counselors abandon the idea of truth? A chapter is devoted to each question. These chapters have the following structure: the issue is introduced; the personal and professional significance of the topic is noted; the question is thoroughly considered; and a discussion of pertinent issues and possible resolutions are presented. Throughout the discussion of these topics, I have disclosed many of the experiences and intellectual struggles that made these ideas important to me. The last chapter summarizes my journey, and the hopes that I have for the future of the helping professions.

Throughout the book, I refer to helping professionals, psychotherapists, therapists, and counselors. The only consideration I used in selecting one of these terms at a particular place in the text was to avoid repetition that might annoy the reader. My doctorate is in clinical psychology, I have been a professor in a department of counseling for nearly twenty years, I married a social worker, and my mother and grandmother were also social workers. Perhaps because of this multi-disciplinary background, I have never been impressed with the argument that sharp distinctions ought to be drawn between the helping professions. Having worked in clinics, agencies, and hospitals for decades, it has been my consistent observation that the various talking therapy professionals, at least in the mental health realm, all do about the same thing. Indeed, there is far more variation among professionals within the same helping profession than there is between the various disciplinary identities. That being said, I have spent the majority of my career as a proud member of the counseling profession. Therefore, I use counseling terminology in the chapter titles and throughout this book with greater frequency than alternative terms that I could have used.

Although I hope that this book is useful and interesting to talking therapists, students, trainees, and educators from various disciplines, it was written with "displaced humanists" (Hansen, 2009a, p. 65) (who can be found in all of the helping professions) in mind. Here are a series of items to help you determine if you are a displaced humanist: (a) you prefer the ambiguity of human meaning systems to the certainty of diagnostics in the helping process; (b) you find the technical aspects of contemporary mental health culture frustrating and long for rich, literary understandings of clients; (c) although you appreciate science, you regard psychotherapy as an art, more akin to the humanities than science; (d) you think of your clients as struggling with understandable problems of living, not as disordered, sick, ill, or deficient; and (e) you are not really sure what you learned in graduate school; you had hoped your training would complicate and dimensionalize your understanding of people, but, instead, you often felt intellectually frustrated because clients were reduced to simple, technique responsive clusters of symptoms.

If any of the above items resonate with you, you are probably a displaced humanist, whose humanistic sensibilities make it difficult to operate in contemporary, technocratic, medicalized mental health culture. I hope that this book, with its forays into the ambiguous, paradoxical, dynamic, nuanced, and philosophical elements of professional life, helps to validate and satisfy your cravings for depth and meaning in your work.

Acknowledgments

Because the content of this book is often presented in the context of my intellectual struggles, the reader may get the impression that the ideas simply sprung forth from my mind, without outside influence. This is absolutely not the case. While I am responsible for the content, I am indebted to a wide network of colleagues, friends, and family who have supported, encouraged, and challenged me throughout my career. However, as my friend and colleague Bob Fink has reminded me, there is a strong oral tradition in the helping professions. This can sometimes make it difficult to remember precisely who to acknowledge, but I am certainly grateful to the people who are noted below.

I am thankful to be a member of the strong intellectual community in the Department of Counseling at Oakland University. I could not wish for better faculty colleagues. I am particularly grateful for the friendship and support of Bob Fink, Lisa Hawley, Todd Leibert, and Phil O'Dwyer. Notably, Luellen Ramey, who served as my departmental chair for the majority of my time at the university, is a dear friend and colleague. I have benefited immensely from her wisdom, guidance, and support.

Prior to writing this book, I initiated and taught an elective course in philosophical topics in counseling. Every time that it was offered, this course was filled with intelligent, enthusiastic students who became strongly engaged with the philosophical ideas. The students asked challenging questions, debated the topics that I presented, and engaged in lively discussions. These experiences with my students undoubtedly contributed to the formation of this book.

Nothing brings ideas to life like working with clients. Theories take on new meaning when they are positioned within the helping encounter. I have certainly learned, benefited, and grown from the new life and meaning that clients have given to the ideas that are presented in this book.

Although I capitalize on the more contradictory and dogmatic elements of my graduate school education to make certain points, I appreciate my former professors and the many valuable things that they taught me. Their influence undoubtedly extends into these pages.

I am grateful to Amy King, my editor at Rowman & Littlefield, who took a chance on what must have seemed like a very unusual book. Throughout the process, Amy has been helpful, responsive, and encouraging. I am grateful for her support.

For innumerable reasons, I am grateful to my parents. My father has always had a strong philosophical mindset. My mother, a social worker, worked as a clinician throughout her career. I am thankful that the philosophical and clinical interests of my parents somehow blended within me to create a wonderful career and this book.

Last, being intensely immersed in a project can have interesting consequences for a family system. I am very grateful for the support of my wife and children. Thank you for coming along on this ride with me.

Chapter One

Mental Health Culture

One of the implicit themes of this book is that ideas always arise out of human minds. It is logically impossible, then, to fully appreciate, and critique ideologies without some knowledge of the meaning systems, quirks, struggles, and biases of the people who proffer them. For instance, when considering psychoanalytic ideas, it is arguably useful to know that Freud thought of himself as a scientist, was generally intolerant of people who disagreed with him, and, as a child, was highly indulged by his mother (Gay, 1988). Knowing these personal features of the founder helps to make sense of diverse components of the psychoanalytic movement, such as the Oedipal conflict, the strict dogmatism of training institutes (Kirsner, 2000), and the naive realism of traditional Freudian ideas. As another example, Rogers' early life on a farm and his seminary training (Kirschenbaum, 2007) give new meaning and context to the humanistic ideals of growth and self-actualization.

Unfortunately, however, it is relatively uncommon for disseminators of ideas to disclose the personal factors that made the ideas important to them. Perhaps many intellectuals are unwilling to admit (even to themselves) that their ideological choices have subjective influences for fear that this acknowledgment would somehow undermine the credibility or perceived objectivity of their positions. Indeed, personal disclosure in the scholarly realm is a rarity. Flip through virtually any academic journal and you will be hard pressed to find a discussion of the personal meaning of the subject matter to the authors.

In contrast to this current standard of scholarly discourse, I have peppered these chapters with self-disclosures, including anecdotes, intellectual struggles, and my best guesses about the reasons that certain ideas became important to me. My hope is that this will provide the reader with a rich, personal vantage point for appreciating and critiquing the ideological positions I advocate. However, knowledge about subjective influences can never provide a complete context for understanding a presentation of ideas. Cultural factors must also be considered.

Personal meaning systems are by-products of the cultures in which they arise; subjectivity sprouts from the soil of culture (Gergen, 1991). At an ideological level, I have frequently observed that the structure of my thinking mirrors the standards of the culture in which I am immersed. I used to be troubled by this observation because I naively aspired to be objective, independent, and free of the confines of culture. Currently, I believe that the best I can do is become aware of cultural influences, reflect on the impact they have had on me, and try to imagine something beyond them.

For example, in graduate school I learned a model of psychotherapy that was designed to help troubled individuals. However, I cannot ever remember questioning the assumption that individuals should be the unit of treatment concern. As proponents of family systems orientations (e.g., Minuchin, 1974) have noted, it is perfectly reasonable to presume that problems reside in systems, not individuals. Once I had been exposed to this systemic position, it seemed completely obvious to me, and I was disappointed that I had not been able to think of it myself. I had been enculturated, both developmentally and in my graduate training, in a strong culture of individualism that had blinded me to other possibilities.

The influence of culture is thoroughgoing and ubiquitous. The psychosexual emphasis in traditional psychoanalysis certainly had its origins, at least in part, from the sexually repressive culture of turn of the century Vienna (Gay, 1988; Makari, 2008). In our current technocratic age, cognitive models built on a metaphor of computer programming, rule the day. The idea that human change can be brought about by reprogramming the hard-drive of the mind with new thoughts has powerful appeal in a culture that places a high value on technology (Hansen, 2007a). On an individual level, the current version of the Diagnostic and Statistical Manual (DSM) (American Psychiatric Association, 2000) has a chapter on culture-bound syndromes, such as "koro" (p. 900), whereby the sufferer, usually a member of Asian culture, believes his genitals are shrinking and will eventually disappear, despite medical evidence to the contrary. Sequestering certain types of problems in a special culture-bound section of the DSM, though, is an intellectually questionable practice that perhaps reveals the ethnocentricity of the authors, given that all human problems arise within cultures and are, thereby, culturally bound.

Some might cite the scientific method as having the ability to identify pristine truths that are beyond cultural influence. Kuhn (1996), however, persuasively argued that scientific investigation is a cultural activity. Training to become a scientist involves an intensive indoctrination into a particular intellectual community, which determines the topics to investigate and the range of acceptable findings. For instance, scientists who operate within the communal culture of biological psychiatry will never conclude that depression is caused by unconscious conflict or irrational thoughts because these conclusions are not acceptable to this community. There is no escaping culture. Even scientific investigations and findings are culturally derived phenomena.

Among other influences, I am a product of mental health culture. Therefore, an understanding of the origins, history, and current state of mental health culture is necessary to provide an adequate context for appraising my intellectual conclusions. I also hope that the following discussion will encourage readers to reflect on the way that they have been influenced by their own cultural immersions. Learning about the historical forces that created one's cultural milieu is the first step to imagining something beyond the surround.

HISTORICAL ORIGINS OF
CONTEMPORARY MENTAL HEALTH CULTURE

In my experience, people often assume that the primary determinants of mental health culture are objective findings, which, every year, bring us closer to some ultimate truth about human psychological suffering. Within this progressive view of history, the understandings of one era are necessarily superior to prior conceptualizations. I do not endorse this view. Certainly, the ability of practitioners to help "suffering strangers" (Orange, 2011, p. 37) has advanced over time in particular realms. It is undoubtedly more effective and humane to treat individuals who suffer from hallucinations with modern medications than by lobotomizing them, for example. However, the view that mental health history represents a progressive climb up some ladder that will eventually lead to definitive answers ignores the money, power, politics, and territorial disputes that have forged the cultural milieu in which practitioners currently operate (Hansen, 2005c).

A discussion of the determinants of contemporary mental health culture could conceivably begin at multiple historical points. However, the asylum movement in the eighteenth th and nineteenth centuries is probably a good place to start. With asylums, mental health treatment became an industry with professionals, treatment models, and government support. These core elements remain components of modern mental health care.

During the 1700s and 1800s, asylums began to dot the landscapes of Europe and America (Shorter, 1997). Unlike modern psychiatric hospitals, these asylums were enormous campuses where people afflicted with madness were housed for years, decades, or even for the duration of their lives. There have been various speculations about the reasons that the asylum movement emerged at this point in history. Foucault (1965), for example, proposed that the end of leprosy in Europe was the key factor. During the leprosy epidemic, huge leprosariums were built to segregate and house the afflicted so that members of the community would not be infected. Once leprosy remitted, Foucault speculated, other undesirables were gradually committed to the empty leprosariums, as European society looked for a new cultural outsider to replace the lepers. Eventually, the structures that formerly housed lepers came to imprison the mad.

Others have noted that capitalism and the asylum movement emerged at about the same time (Reiss, 2008). In capitalist economies people who cannot participate in the workforce are problematic. Perhaps the invention of mental illness and asylums was a way to manage this problem by labeling nonworkers as deviant and sequestering them in special housing. The mental health industry, from this perspective, is simply the handmaiden of capitalism (Parker, 2007).

Whatever the reasons for the asylum movement, it gained strong momentum during the 1800s, as the burgeoning industry began to take shape (Shorter, 1997). During this movement, and indeed, throughout mental health history, two explanatory models dominated expert attempts to account for the disorders of asylum residents: (1) biological and (2) psychosocial (Hansen, 2009a). Because these models have virtually defined the evolution of ideas, have persisted throughout history, and, even today, shape mental health culture, they are worth reviewing.

The biological model posits that mental problems are ultimately the result of biological abnormalities (Shorter, 1997). This model serves as the ideological foundation of the contemporary psychiatric search for neurotransmitter and brain based abnormalities to account for depression, schizophrenia, and other disorders. Arguably, however, it was not until the mid-twentieth century that medical interventions produced true help for psychiatric patients (Shorter, 1997). Throughout the history of psychiatry, biological hypotheses have yielded bizarre, barbaric, and damaging methods for treating asylum residents (Whitaker, 2002).

For instance, during the early 1800s a spinning chair device was patented as a way to treat psychiatric patients. The unfortunate recipient of this treatment would be strapped into the chair, which was then hoisted above the ground and swung and rotated rapidly (Whitaker, 2002). Other ninteenth century biological treatments involved the chemical induction of sleep for multiple days in a row and surgical removal of the intestines (Shorter, 1997; Whitaker, 2002). Indeed, the evolution of these supposed treatments followed a similar pattern, which, arguably, can still be observed in mental health culture today, albeit in a moderated form: (a) a powerful, influential figure formulates a theory about the cause of and treatment for mental health problems based on scant, observational evidence; (b) the treatment is widely implemented throughout the domain of the person who came up with the idea; (c) the treatment is deemed to be effective, as professional observers interpret all post-treatment signs as indications of success, despite obvious evidence that would lead virtually anyone to conclude that it had been a colossal failure;(d) there is a gradual disillusionment and subsequent abandonment of the treatment, as professionals observe its ineffectiveness and tragic flaws; and (e) a new treatment comes into vogue and the cycle begins again.

As an interesting historical example of some of the elements of this process, Freud's friend and colleague, Wilhelm Fleiss, firmly believed, and propagated the idea, that the source of mental health problems was nasal abnormalities (Masson, 1984). At an early point in his career, Freud referred some of his patients to Fleiss, who performed nasal surgery on them. Unfortunately for his patients, Fleiss' theory was not only bizarrely misguided, but he was a surgical hack. At least one of Freud's patients who received nasal surgery from Fleiss suffered from profuse, life-threatening nasal bleeding over an extended period of time. Freud, perhaps not wanting to offend Fleiss or jeopardize his relationship with him, claimed that the woman's bleeding was caused by a hysterical conversion reaction, not Fleiss' knife (Masson, 1984).

In contrast to the biological model, the psychosocial models of treatment posit that mental health problems are psychologically based (Hansen, 2009a; Whitaker, 2002). During the asylum era, future reformers would observe the barbaric conditions of the asylums, such as residents being chained to walls. These observations led to reform movements and humane forms of treatment (Whitaker, 2002). Various types of therapeutic communities were subsequently established (e.g., Jones, 1953) wherein, patient governances allowed residents to play an active role in determining the conditions of their asylum life. To promote pride and a sense of purpose, residents were assigned various duties and jobs on the asylum campus. Advocates of the psychosocial model presumed that humane treatment, a sense of community, and the various activities, which engendered meaning and purpose in the lives of asylum residents, would be curative (Whitaker, 2002).

Like the biological model, the idea that mental health problems originate from social or psychological sources has been active throughout the history of the helping professions (Hansen, 2009a; Shorter, 1997). The contemporary cognitive-behavioral model of treatment, for example, is based on the presumption that faulty thinking, not biological abnormalities, is the cause of psychological suffering (Mahoney, 1991). Cure, from the cognitive perspective, involves reframing a client's thoughts so that they no longer cause emotional or behavioral difficulties.

This psychosocial model, although a welcome reprieve from the barbarism of early biological interventions, has also generated its own bizarre and harmful forms of treatment. Bettleheim, for example, promulgated the idea that autism was caused by cold, refrigerator mothers, who were at fault for their child's condition (Pollak, 1997). No one was cured of autism with this psychological theory, and mothers suffered from intense guilt over what they had presumably done to their children. Early followers of Melanie Klein interpreted their adult client's symptoms according to the bizarre tenets of Kleinian theory, such as unconscious hate and envy of the breast from which they were fed as infants (Grosskurth, 1987). Primal scream therapy achieved a popular following during the early 1970s. Patients were told that their problems were the result of repressed, bottled-up emotions, which could only be released by extended cathartic screaming. When it was introduced, primal scream therapy was idealized as a cure for neurosis (Janov, 1970).

Biological and psychosocial visions of professional helping have each made helpful contributions to the understanding and treatment of human emotional suffering. However, these paradigms have also generated numerous bizarre and harmful treatment approaches. Interestingly, throughout history, when one of these overarching views is culturally dominant, the other is relatively submerged (Hansen, 2009a). Ideally, biological and psychosocial ideologies should join forces, so that mental health culture might benefit equally from the insights of both of these meta-perspectives. However, as I demonstrate in the subsequent historical discussion, this ideological equality has never been the case. When the biological model has been dominant, the psychosocial model has been virtually ignored, and vice versa. Therefore, it is inaccurate to depict the history of mental health culture has strictly progressive. This history can be better characterized as a swinging pendulum, which regularly alternates between psychosocial and biological perspectives (Hansen, 2009a).

The historical factors that would cause the pendulum to swing strongly in the psychosocial direction began to take shape during the late nineteenth century (Makari, 2008; Shorter, 1997). Specifically, Sigmund Freud, the inventor of psychoanalysis, had a profound impact on mental health culture for decades to come. Freud was a neurologist, who, because of widespread anti-Semitism in turn of the century Vienna, was prevented from becoming a university research professor. In order to provide for his family, Freud had to work as a practicing neurologist, a relatively undesirable career choice to him, given his aspirations to make great scientific discoveries (Gay, 1988).

Turn-of-the-century neurology was an entirely different profession than it is today. Essentially, neurologists in Freud's time treated patients with nervous conditions (Shorter, 1997). Today these problems would be referred to as mental health disorders. However, during the late 1800s, many presumed that the disorders originated in the nervous system, which meant that neurologists were the appropriate doctors to treat them. Freud treated Viennese women who were diagnosed with hysteria, and many of his patients had physical symptoms that did not have any medical explanation (Makari, 2008;

Masson, 1984). For example, glove paralysis was a term used to describe the inability to move one's hand. The medical professionals of the time knew that it was physiologically impossible for the hand to be subject to paralysis when the arms were fully functional (McWilliams, 1999). There must be some psychological component, professionals reasoned, behind the symptom.

This psychological hypothesis about conversion reactions was strengthened by the work of Charcot, a French hypnotist who demonstrated that paralysis could be hypnotically induced (Makari, 2008). This led Freud to adopt hypnosis as a treatment for his patients. Ultimately, however, Freud became dissatisfied with the effectiveness of hypnosis and subsequently abandoned it as a treatment method (Gay, 1988).

The diverse historical factors that facilitated the emergence of psychoanalysis are complex and beyond the scope of this discussion. Suffice it to say that a mixture of post-Charcot excitement about the psychogenic origins of disorders, Freud's scientific disposition and experience with his patients, and Freud's analysis of his own dreams came together in a unique ideological blend to form psychoanalysis (Gay, 1988; Makari, 2008). The central, early tenets of this new form of treatment were that (a) everyone has a rich unconscious mental life; consciousness is just the tip of the psychic iceberg; (b) psychosexual conflicts from childhood are actively repressed into the unconscious; (c) these conflicts are charged with psychic energy (i.e., libido), which can cause them to reemerge in disguised, derivative form as symptoms; and (d) by using the psychoanalytic method, practitioners can reveal and help patients work through the unconscious determinants of their symptoms, thereby promoting cure (Gay, 1988; Makari, 2008; Pine, 1990).

At first, Freud's ideas were dismissed as quackery by the medical establishment, although psychoanalytic ideology initially attracted a wide range of Viennese intellectuals, such as artists, writers, and doctors (Makari, 2008). Gradually, as psychoanalysis became institutionalized in the early 1900s, a core group of treatment professionals became devoted followers of Freudian ideas. The movement began to gain strong momentum and spread to other regions as the new century progressed (Makari, 2008). As psychoanalysis became more influential, the ideological pendulum began to swing in the psychosocial direction (Hansen, 2009a).

Psychoanalysis was introduced to the United States in the early 1900s, particularly when Freud was invited to speak about his work at Clark University in 1909 (Makari, 2008). However, during the 1930s the increasing threat of Nazi occupation caused founding psychoanalysts, most of whom were Jews, to flee to the United States (Jacoby, 1983; Makari, 2008; Shorter, 1997). These foreign psychoanalysts took university appointments and established psychoanalytic institutes, thereby spreading Freudian ideas throughout American culture. Once psychoanalysis hit American soil, psychiatrists immediately took hold of it and banned other professionals from becoming psychoanalytic practitioners (Shorter, 1997). This psychiatric lock on psychoanalysis was never intended by Freud, who promoted the idea that various professionals should become psychoanalysts (Freud, 1926/1959). Until they were defeated in a lawsuit in 1986, the psychiatric guild successfully banned other professionals from enrolling in formal psychoanalytic institute training (McWilliams, 2004).

As a personal aside, Richard Sterba (1982), a member of the core group of early Viennese psychoanalysts, immigrated to the Detroit area and subsequently established a strong relationship with the Clinical Psychology Department of the University of Detroit, where I received my graduate training. During one of my classes, the program director asked for volunteers to move furniture at Dr. Sterba's home. Wanting to meet this aging icon of psychoanalysis, I jumped at the chance. Dr. Sterba was warm, friendly, and eager to talk about his experiences with Freud and the early psychoanalysts. In fact, he showed me his graduate certificate from the Viennese psychoanalytic institute, which was signed by Freud. Shortly after signing this certificate, Dr. Sterba explained, Freud stopped signing certificates altogether to appease graduates of institutes from other regions who were upset that they were not able to obtain Freud's signature on their certificates. While I was there, Bruno Bettleheim, another icon of the early psychoanalytic movement, called. I overheard Dr. Sterba have an extended conversation in German with his colleague. I am still awestruck by the way that psychoanalytic history came to life for me on that day.

Returning to the historical account, American mental health culture was gradually overtaken by psychoanalysis throughout the 1940s and 1950s (Makari, 2008; Shorter, 1997), which caused the ideological pendulum to swing strongly in the direction of psychological explanations for mental health problems (Hansen, 2009a). Indeed, to be an elite psychiatrist during this era, one had to undergo extensive, post-graduate psychoanalytic training. Biological psychiatrists continued to attempt supposed treatments with asylum residents, such as dunking in cold baths and insulin shock (Shorter, 1997; Whitaker, 2002). However, these biological psychiatrists had a richly deserved reputation for quackery and were looked down upon by the elite psychoanalytic psychiatrists. One of the most horrific and damaging failures of the biological psychiatrists in the mid-twentieth century was lobotomy.

Lobotomy is a crude psychosurgical procedure designed to treat psychosis through partial destruction of the frontal lobes (Shorter, 1997; Whitaker, 2002). In their blind, irrational exuberance over lobotomy, biological psychiatrists noted that the procedure often caused a remission of psychotic symptoms but somehow missed the fact that the unfortunate recipients of this cure usually became vacant, incontinent zombies. Indeed, despite its tragic effects Antonio Moniz, the founder of lobotomy, was awarded a Nobel Prize for inventing the procedure (Whitaker, 2002). Perhaps the most famous recipient of this treatment was Rosemary Kennedy, the sister of John F. Kennedy (Szasz, 2007a). In the context of a highly successful, powerful family, Joseph Kennedy was perhaps embarrassed by his daughter, who, by all accounts, had a lively personality but was intellectually a bit slow. The Kennedy patriarch found a psychiatrist willing to perform a lobotomy on Rosemary. After the procedure, Rosemary was permanently disabled and spent the remainder of her life being cared for in a residential facility (Szasz, 2007a).

During the 1950s, then, the dominance of psychoanalytic explanations for mental health problems caused the ideological pendulum to be fixed in the psychosocial position. Biological explanations were suppressed by this cultural emphasis on psychoanalytic ideology. Contemporarily, the opposite is arguably the case; the medical model is rampant and psychological explanations are suppressed. Psychiatry has become an exclusively biologically based, medical profession, and it is exceedingly rare for a modern psychiatrist to use psychotherapeutic treatment interventions (Whitaker, 2002). Indeed, even psychotherapy and counseling are structured by a strict medical model, with diagnosis, treatment plans, and symptom based outcome measures (Hansen, 2007d). There are several historical factors that caused this massive swing of the pendulum in the past half-century.

First, biological psychiatrists finally found effective, although crude by contemporary standards, treatments for mental health problems (Shorter, 1997). Thorazine, lithium, antidepressants, and antianxiety agents were introduced in the 1950s and 1960s. Thorazine, a major tranquilizer, decreased psychotic symptoms, although its chronic use eventually results in debilitating neurological side effects (i.e., tardive dyskinesia). Lithium, a naturally occurring salt, was a godsend for those afflicted with manic-depression, a condition whereby the sufferer is afflicted with extreme mood alterations, from dark, suicidal, depressive lows to exuberant, grandiose, and sometimes psychotic, manic highs. For arguably the first time in history, biological psychiatrists discovered treatments that did more good than harm (Fancher, 1995; Shorter, 1997).

Second, beginning in the 1950s research psychologists (e.g., Eysenck, 1952; Eysenck & Wilson, 1973) challenged the effectiveness of psychoanalysis. Academic researchers argued that psychoanalytic treatment was no better than a placebo. The psychoanalytic royalty generally scoffed at these findings, claiming that the rich personality changes brought about by psychoanalysis could not possibly be captured by the reductive quantitative methods of the research psychologists. Eventually, however, the outcome research contributed to a weakening of psychoanalytic dominance (Hansen, 2009a; Shorter, 1997).

Third, competitive treatments emerged, particularly from psychologists. By the 1950s, behavioral psychologists had been conducting experiments with rats and pigeons within universities for decades. Because they were successful at changing animal behavior in a laboratory, it was reasonable for behaviorists to conclude that they could use the same principles to change human behavior in a therapy office. For instance, Wolpe (1958), who theorized that phobias are the result of a classically conditioned response between anxiety and a phobic object or situation, developed systematic desensitization, a therapeutic procedure designed to incrementally expose clients to the source of their fears while inducing a relaxation response. Because relaxation is incompatible with anxiety, the phobia would eventually be eliminated by this treatment method. Consumers of mental health services could now choose whether to quickly and effectively eliminate their phobia with behavioral methods, or to initiate costly meetings with a psychoanalyst, multiple times a week for many years, to discuss the supposed psychosexual conflicts lurking behind their fears. The psychoanalysts claimed that mere behavioral elimination of the surface phobia would leave the underlying conflict intact. In other words, because only the surface weed was removed, the conflictual roots would eventually grow new symptoms. However, no credible research evidence emerged to substantiate this symptom substitution hypothesis.

Other treatment methods began to proliferate in mental health culture, thereby further undermining the dominance of psychoanalysis. Ellis, who posited that irrational cognitions were the cause of emotional and behavioral problems, developed Rational Emotive Behavior Therapy (Ellis & Grieger, 1977), a treatment designed to help clients systematically examine and change their flawed patterns of thinking. The existential-humanistic movement emphasized unreduced, authentic relational encounters with clients (DeCarvalho, 1990). Psychotherapists from this tradition helped clients by establishing certain "necessary and sufficient" (Rogers, 1957, p. 95) relational conditions during the therapeutic encounter. This humanistic, or third-force, movement spawned other treatment approaches, such as encounter groups (Elkins, 2009) and Gestalt therapy (Perls, 1969).

Gradually, through licensure legislation, psychologists, social workers, and counselors gained legal privileges to serve as psychotherapy treatment providers (Fancher, 1995). This new competition in the mental health marketplace, research attacks on the effectiveness of psychoanalysis, and the rise of biological psychiatry all contributed to the gradual decline of psychoanalysis in the 1960s and 1970s. Psychiatrists began to give up psychoanalysis for drug therapy, which would eventually prove to be a far more lucrative way to make a living than by engaging in psychoanalytic practice (Shorter, 1997). The ideological pendulum had begun to swing in the biological direction (Hansen, 2009a).

This burgeoning biological psychiatry movement was strongly solidified by the introduction of a new Diagnostic and Statistical Manual (DSM) in 1980. Throughout the history of their profession, psychiatrists had attempted to model their practices after other areas of medicine (Shorter, 1997). A diagnostic guide is fundamental to medical practice and, psychiatrists had hoped that a manual of psychiatric disorders would serve to legitimize psychiatry as an authentic, medical profession. The first DSM was introduced in 1952, but this version, and a subsequent one released decades later, was virtually ignored by mental health practitioners. These early editions were ideologically tied to psychoanalytic hypotheses about mental health disorders (Shorter, 1997).

During the 1970s, Robert Sptizer, a psychiatrist, professionally devoted himself to the creation of the next version of the DSM (Spiegel, 2005). Rather than base this new diagnostic manual on psychoanalytic ideology, Spitzer chose to revive descriptive psychiatry, a nosological movement that had been largely dormant since the late nineteenth century, to serve as the ideological foundation for the new DSM (Mayes & Horwitz, 2005; Shorter, 1997). The basic tenet of descriptive psychiatry is that mental health disorders should be categorized according to symptoms alone, without any ties to theoretical orientations. The presumed advantage of this atheoretical, classificatory approach is that professionals from diverse orientations can easily communicate with each other about clients. Furthermore, it was hoped that a purely descriptive guide would facilitate mental health research by specifying reliable diagnostic categories that are homogenous with regard to symptoms (Mayes & Horwitz, 2005; Shorter, 1997). As I note below in my critiques of the DSM, this initial vision of the manual was naive and did not live up to its promises. However, the introduction of the DSM-III in 1980 was a monumental moment in the history of mental health culture. Practitioners and the public alike began to take psychiatric diagnostics seriously (Mayes & Horwitz, 2005).

Another important trend that contributed to the formation of a new mental health culture during the 1980s was that health care reimbursement for mental health services began to become dictated by the principles of managed care (Hansen, 1997; Morris, 1994). Tired of paying lavishly for interminable treatments, insurance companies demanded that practitioners focus their efforts on reducing symptoms, not on changing personality structures. This managed care model required mental health treatments to be micromanaged by third-party gatekeepers, who held practitioners accountable for demonstrating progress in the form of symptom amelioration. A trifecta of powerful forces, then, combined in the 1980s to cause the ideological pendulum to swing hard in the biological, medical direction: (a) the introduction of a symptom based diagnostic guide; (b) managed care control of reimbursement for mental health services; and (c) the pharmaceutical industry pouring billions of dollars into the development and marketing of psychiatric medications (Murray, 2009). The synergy of these forces created a powerful wave of medicalization. Psychiatrists abandoned talking therapy in droves and adopted far more lucrative medication-based practices (Shorter, 1997).

Not wanting to be left out of the economic rewards and status of this new medicalization, talking therapists began successfully billing managed care insurance companies for psychotherapy and counseling. Although this move was financially beneficial for nonpsychiatric practitioners, reimbursement for treatment came with a host of stipulations from managed care companies. In addition to micromanaging psychotherapy and requiring excessive amounts of documentation, managed care companies also demanded that practitioners characterize treatment in medicalized terms. Therapists began acquiescing to these demands and the language of medicalization began to overtake the helping professions. Psychotherapists increasingly began talking like physicians, using the language of disorders, symptoms, and treatment plans (Elkins, 2009; Hansen, 2005a; Hansen, 2007b)

During the 1990s, these trends accelerated. To add fuel to this medical fire, pharmaceutical companies gained the legal right to market directly to consumers. Prior to the mid-1990s direct advertising of prescription medication to consumers was highly restricted by law (Ventola, 2011). Once these restrictions were lifted, however, television, popular magazines, and other media outlets aggressively promoted the positive effects of psychiatric medication. Formerly depressed people happily skipping through fields after taking antidepressants and similar marketing campaigns proved to be powerfully persuasive to the public. The patient-doctor dynamic shifted. Instead of physicians advising patients to take particular drugs, patients placed pressure on their doctors to prescribe new medications.

Multiple personal experiences have convinced me of the effectiveness of this psychiatric-pharmaceutical marketing campaign. However, two experiences stand out as particularly significant. In the mid-2000s, my son, who was probably about eight years old at the time, had an upsetting day at school and asked me to get him some medication. He had never taken medication before, except during brief periods when he had been ill. Upon exploring his request further, I learned that he had recently seen an advertisement for antidepressants on television. Having been raised within a medical-psychiatric culture, he thought it perfectly reasonable to ask for pills after a bad day.

On another occasion, I showed up for my weekly consulting job at a local clinic and settled into my office, which was used by a child psychiatrist when I was not there. I was horrified and disillusioned to discover that the office, which had been relatively bare the week before, was now littered with toy-like items bearing pharmaceutical drug logos. I understand that the pharmaceutical industry has a right to market directly to consumers, but decorating Legos and other toys designed for five-year-olds with cartoon like characters pushing pills is a practice that, to me, crosses an ethical line.

In the early 1990s, psychologists, perhaps out of a fear that their profession might be rendered obsolete by the increasing dominance of biological psychiatry, began to structure their research methods according to the medical model. Psychologists hoped to adopt a psychiatric model of practice by identifying specific psychotherapeutic treatments that would work best with particular disorders (Wampold, 2001). With this model of research, psychologists aspired to have their own prescriptions, in the form of particular types of therapies, to treat disorders, just like their medical colleagues. This new, prescriptive, medicalized way of conceptualizing and structuring psychotherapy outcome research further ensconced the talking professions into the medical model (Hansen, 2006d; Messer & Wampold, 2002). There were multiple ideological and practical flaws with this empirically validated treatment movement (Marquis & Douhit, 2006; Wampold, 2001) that are covered in future chapters. For purposes of this discussion, however, suffice it to say that this research trend, along with biological psychiatry, reimbursement pressures from managed care, the powerful financial influence of the pharmaceutical industry, and the cultural dominance of the new, descriptive DSM, caused the ideological pendulum to swing strongly in the biological, medical direction, where it has remained to this day (Hansen, 2009a).

It is interesting to speculate about when the pendulum might swing back to a psychosocial view of mental health problems. Indeed, using history as a guide, mental health culture is probably overdue for a psychosocial correction. Why, then, has this medicalized trend only accelerated over the past few decades, when ordinarily it would have yielded to psychosocial ideologies by now? A reasonable answer to this question is that there is an important factor that makes this era unique: The power of the pharmaceutical industry (Murray, 2009). Unlike other times in mental health history, there are now billions of dollars to be made by keeping the ideological pendulum on the medical side. I have never seen an advertisement on television, or any other mass media outlet, extolling the benefits of psychotherapy. However, it is difficult to go through a day without being exposed to multiple advertisements for psychiatric medications. In this era, money arguably keeps the pendulum stuck in the medical position. Given these powerful economic incentives, it is difficult to determine if it will ever swing back to the psychosocial side.

Mental health culture, then, is not strictly progressive, with objectively better treatments and understandings emerging year after year. If current practices were always superior to the practices of the past era, practitioners would simply have to blindly follow contemporary cultural mandates to deliver the best and most advanced care. However, because mental health culture is significantly determined by money, politics, territorial disputes among professions, diagnostic and treatment faddism, and ideological swings between various conceptualizations of human problems, practitioners have a duty to think critically about the dictates of the current culture (Hansen, 2005c).

In this regard, there have been regrettable trends during every period of mental health history. Lobotomy, classifying homosexuality as a mental illness, and the repressed memories movement of the 1980s are just a few examples of the many harmful trends that have occurred during the twentieth century. It is a useful exercise in critical thought, then, to consider which current practices and conceptualizations might be considered misguided decades from now. Every past era has had cultural standards that were mistaken and harmful, so it is naive to think that the present era would be an exception. My favorite candidate for the current practice that will be considered the most regrettable in the future is the mass psychiatric drugging of children. However, there are undoubtedly multiple contemporary trends, which students are taught and practitioners implement, that, in retrospect, will be considered misguided and harmful. To promote critical thinking, I encourage readers to continually think about which modern trends might be seen as regrettable in the future. Engaging in this exercise makes one less likely to blindly follow current practices. Indeed, it may even cause one to envision something better, beyond the realm of contemporary mental health culture.

CRITIQUE OF CONTEMPORARY MENTAL HEALTH CULTURE

As noted above, contemporary mental health culture is guided by the medical model, which has ideologically saturated current conceptual models and treatment paradigms. Given its dominance, an important component of the following discussion is a critique of the medical model and the concomitant conceptualization of psychotherapists and counselors as health care professionals. Prior to beginning this discussion, however, it is important to distinguish between the medical model as an ideology and medication as a treatment intervention.

Although arguably overprescribed in contemporary times, psychiatric medications have alleviated the suffering of countless individuals over the past half-century (Shorter, 1997). I know many people who have benefited from psychiatric medication, and I regularly refer clients to psychiatrists when talking therapy alone is insufficient to help them. In my critique below, then, I am not taking a stance against medication or the psychiatric profession. Furthermore, I am not critiquing the medical model in and of itself. Conceptual models are tools. As such, they can only be evaluated in terms of their utility for performing certain tasks. Arguing that the medical model is intrinsically good or bad would be tantamount to making comprehensive statements about hammers, microprocessors, or the periodic table of elements. Tools cannot be evaluated apart from use cases. The periodic table of elements is indispensable for chemists, but useless for architects. My primary critique of the medical model, then, is that it is employed in realms (i.e., psychotherapy and counseling) where it has no benefit or is outright harmful.

It would be nonsensical to disparage any model apart from linking it to particular uses.

Over the years I have learned to begin my critique with these clarifying remarks. Otherwise, people erroneously tend to believe that I am against psychiatric medication, have some axe to grind with the psychiatric profession, or want the medical model to be banned. None of these are the case. That being said, I can proceed to a critical examination of the idea that talking therapy is a form of health care.

Talking Therapy as Health Care

During the 1980s, it was my observation that talking therapists strongly resented the demand to describe their work in medicalized terms but reluctantly did so to get paid. Over the past three decades, however, I believe that therapists have increasingly taken pride in identifying themselves as pseudo-medical professionals. Indeed, nowadays it is common for psychotherapists and counselors to regard themselves as health care providers (Hansen, 2007d). This identification with health care is continually demonstrated to me when I supervise new practitioners, many of whom are trained to strongly value the DSM, the construction of symptom-based treatment plans, and the technical elements of therapy. They are usually disillusioned when I tell them that this knowledge base has little to do with the elements of effective relational helping, such as intimacy, safety, a sense of alliance, and gut-wrenching emotional honesty.

It is very counterintuitive, indeed, that a health care identity has been so firmly established for professionals who practice talking therapy. Whenever I have looked into any psychotherapy office at the numerous clinics and agencies where I have practiced over the past two decades, I have never seen stethoscopes, syringes, blood pressure cuffs, or any other medical paraphernalia. These offices are simply equipped with some chairs and perhaps a desk. The psychotherapy space is clearly designed for talking, not some medical, health care procedure.

To extend this argument, suppose a visitor from another planet, who had no familiarity with earthly professions, were to observe a lawyer, accountant, counselor, and real estate broker at work with clients in their offices. The alien would then be provided with a brief description of each of the professions, such as accountants assist people with managing money and counselors help people with problems of living. Then, this cosmic visitor would observe a medical professional, such as a physician, perhaps doing surgery or applying a cast to a broken leg. At this point, the alien would be told that one of the first professions is conceptualized as health care, just like the medical profession. I do not think that this interplanetary visitor would have any basis for determining which of the first professions is considered health care. I imagine that the alien would respond that each of the first professions simply consists of two earthlings talking; there is nothing about any of them that resembles the activities of the medical professionals.

Despite the fact that there are no obvious similarities between the professional activities of talking therapists and medical personnel, there are at least two justifications that are can be used to categorize counseling and psychotherapy as health care professions. I have discussed these justifications, and my arguments against them, more extensively elsewhere (Hansen, 2007d). However, they are worth reviewing here.

The first argument is based on the reasonable assumption that the mind and body should be viewed holistically, not as separate entities. This is surely a sensible position, as stress, for example, can cause medical problems and exercise can sharpen one's mental capacities. The metaphysical separation of mind and body, which has been a part of the Western intellectual tradition for centuries (Stolorow, Atwood & Orange, 2002), should, indeed, probably be abandoned. However, some might leverage this rejection of mind-body dualism to argue that counseling should be considered a healthcare profession because counseling can cause observable changes to the brain and a reduction of physical symptoms.

The abandonment of mind-body dualism, however, does not logically necessitate that counseling should be described as a medical, health care profession. Indeed, many, arguably all, talking professions have an impact on the body (Hansen, 2007d). For example, suppose someone is experiencing severe stress over financial matters with accompanying bodily symptoms, such as ulcers. After obtaining help from an accountant, however, the financial stress is alleviated and the ulcers disappear. Through talking, the accountant cured the ulcers. Furthermore, a scan of the client's brain would surely reveal changes due to this professional intervention. Should accountants be considered health care professionals, then? What about lawyers, teachers, and other talking professionals who have a similar impact on their clientele? The end of mind-body dualism, therefore, does not necessitate that counselors or psychotherapists should be considered health care professionals, unless all other talking professionals are also placed in this category (Hansen, 2007d). Of course, it would be meaningless and absurd to categorize all professions as health care. It is far more sensible to reserve the medical, health care category for professionals who directly intervene in the realm of bodily processes.

As a second reason for classifying counseling as health care, some might argue that the clients of counselors usually have diagnosable, psychiatric disorders. Because psychiatry is a medical profession, and counselors treat clients with psychiatric disorders, counseling, by extension, should be considered a medical, health care profession. The primary problem with this argument is that there is no justification to classify most psychiatric disorders as medical, health care problems. Virtually none of the DSM disorders have biological markers (Frances, 2009). Indeed, many of the DSM disorders were formerly considered moral or legal problems. However, through psychiatric expansionism, these problems have been reclassified as health care problems (Hansen, 2007d).

As an anecdote to illustrate this point, I formerly worked at a clinic that offered an anger management group. This group typically consisted of court-ordered men, most of whom had assaulted their wives. The counselors who worked with these men routinely diagnosed them with "Intermittent Explosive Disorder" (American Psychiatric Association, 2000, p. 663), which identified these group members as having a health care problem. In passing, the group leader mentioned to me that one of the regular attendees of her group, who had seemed to be making progress, had recently been arrested for assaulting his wife. Unable to resist the opportunity, I made a remark, which may sound insensitive when I present it here, but, in the context of the greater conversation, did not come across as callous. I asked the group leader if, in response to the incident, she had sent a card or flowers. The counselor, caught off guard, said that she had not thought to send anything to the victim of the assault. Correcting her, I asked if she had sent flowers or a card to the group member who had committed the assault. After all, his illness had flared up. When someone who has a health care problem, like cancer, takes a turn for the worse, it is appropriate to respond with sympathy, not with an arrest. In my opinion, a reasonable litmus test for determining whether a problem should be classified as a health care issue is whether it would seem appropriate to send flowers or a get well card to the afflicted person if the problem were to worsen.

Oppositional-defiant disorder, alcoholism, and pediophilia, are just a few examples of so-called disorders that were formerly classified as moral or legal problems. In a prior era, adolescents who committed crimes and regularly disobeyed their parents, for example, had a moral, and perhaps a legal, problem. Contemporarily, due to psychiatric expansionism, these adolescents now have oppositional-defiant disorder, a diagnosis that places these behaviors in the health care domain. Throughout the history of their profession, psychiatrists have gradually transferred problems that were formerly defined as moral or legal into the health care arena (Chodoff, 2002; Hansen, 2007d; Shorter, 1997; Szasz, 1970). Indeed, there was a recent initiative to establish racism as a psychiatric disorder in the new DSM (Guindon, Green & Hanna, 2003). Although this idea may sound absurd now, after racism had been established as a health care problem for several years, people would begin to think of it as a medical disorder, just as oppositional behavior in adolescence is now widely regarded as a health care problem that requires mental health treatment.

If psychiatry had made great advances in addressing problems that were formerly in the moral or legal domain, I would have no objections to psychiatric expansionism. However, there is no evidence that medicalizing moral and legal problems has had any beneficial effect. The only impact of this expansionism is to provide greater power, control, and financial rewards to psychiatry, and, by extension, to the talking therapy professions that have followed psychiatry down this medical path.

Therefore, the argument that counselors and psychotherapists should be considered health care professionals because their clients have medical, psychiatric diagnoses is deeply flawed. The clients of talking therapists have problems of living, which have been medicalized by the forces of psychiatric expansionism. For status and financial gain, counselors and psychotherapists have simply followed psychiatry in this mass medicalization of human problems (Hansen, 2005a). However, this transfer of moral and legal problems into the health care domain cannot possibly serve to justify the classification of talking therapists as medical personnel.

It is logically unjustifiable, then, for counselors and psychotherapists to be considered health care providers. It is important to expose the flaws in reasoning that lead to this health care conclusion because of the numerous harmful consequences that medicalizing the talking therapy professions creates. Specifically, classifying talking therapists as health care professionals automatically shifts the treatment emphasis from relationships to techniques.

Medical personnel heal by implementing prescriptive treatments for particular disorders. This model works well for physicians. When I consult my primary care physician, I expect him to diagnose my problem and prescribe a treatment that has proven effectiveness. However, this prescriptive matching of treatment techniques to particular diagnoses is not an effective strategy for talking therapists. In this regard, Wampold (2001), in an exhaustive review of meta-analytic outcome studies, concluded that techniques account for less than 1 percent of the variance in treatment outcomes. The treatment alliance, and certain features associated with the context of psychotherapy, which are reviewed later in this book, has the highest within-treatment association with outcomes. Therefore, the primary problem with the medicalization of counseling and psychotherapy is that relatively ineffective treatment paradigms are promoted, while the factors that are actually responsible for positive outcomes are trivialized or altogether ignored (Hansen, 2005a).

Medicalization also leads psychotherapists to regard clients as disordered instead of as persons who are struggling with problems of living. This medical emphasis on client disorder and deficiency causes counselors to emphasize guidance, monitoring, advice giving, and case management as primary interventions (Hansen, 2005a). While these interventions certainly have their place, the dominant health care ideology has idealized them, thereby suppressing a therapeutic stance that regards clients as independent, nondeficient adults who can arrive at their own conclusions with the facilitative help of a therapeutic relationship.

Perhaps worse yet, clients may come to think of themselves as broken, deficient beings when they are given a mental health diagnosis. For all of the psychiatric research on pharmaceuticals and brain chemistry, there has been virtually no exploration of the symbolic impact of telling someone that they have a mental illness that requires lifelong pharmaceutical treatment. Throughout my career, I have known clients who have given up on changing, citing the fact that their mental illness has fated them to an unfulfilling existence. While working in inpatient psychiatry, I have often seen children and adolescents blame their outbursts on "my bipolar disorder." Few interactions have saddened me more than listening to the perspective of young children who firmly believe that they are irreparably broken because expert professionals told them that they have a disabling mental disorder, which requires lifelong treatment.

Notably, there is virtually no evidence for the chemical imbalance theory of psychiatric disorders (Whitaker, 2010), despite what patients are routinely told. Because some of the medications that are designed to impact neurotransmitters are effective, it is presumed that the culprit behind psychiatric problems might be brain-based, chemical imbalances. In the future, chemical imbalances or other physiological or genetic causes for severe, stereotypic mental health disorders might be discovered. In the meantime, the practice of telling patients that their problems are completely brain based is clinically irresponsible. Clearly, a host of factors contribute to psychiatric problems, regardless of what future discoveries might reveal.

In this regard, I formerly conducted testing and assessment evaluations on a child and adolescent inpatient psychiatric unit. When there was a significant question about the diagnosis or optimal treatment for a particular child, I was called. I would go to the unit, interview the patient, review the history, administer my tests, and submit a report. In the latter period of my employment in this capacity, unit personnel often asked me to determine if a particular child had bipolar disorder. Inevitably, the child in question, who was often as young as five years old, had a horrendous, traumatic past, full of abuse, multiple foster care placements, poverty, and a history of being cared for by neglectful, addicted parents. These children often had violent tantrums that alternated with periods of irritability or sadness, symptoms that superficially resemble the mood swings of adults who are diagnosed with bipolar disorder.

However, I was always struck by the absurdity of the referral question. Out of all the factors in the lives of these children, how was it that the diagnostic question rose to supreme importance? Over time, I hypothesized a speculative answer. Perhaps the psychiatric profession serves to protect the

public from facing horrific social, family, and systemic problems. It is reassuring to have a profession of experts reduce these larger, seemingly insurmountable problems to brain chemistry. It is as if psychiatrists, by collapsing
all problems into individual brains, have eased the minds of the public by
encouraging them to ignore abuse, poverty, trauma, neglect, addiction, and
other overwhelming systemic and social problems. Do not worry about these
larger social issues, the psychiatric profession implicitly and reassuringly
contends. The only problem is disordered, individual brains. Rather than
challenge the experts, the public has gladly colluded with this reasoning,
reassured that psychiatrists, with their brain-based ideology, have everything
under control.

Not wanting to participate in this collusion, I ordinarily emphasized the
traumatic past of the child and the need for intense psychotherapeutic forms
of treatment in my evaluation reports. I also highlighted the role of parental
responsibility and the importance of changing the system in which the child
was immersed. Regarding the referral question, I usually said that the diagnosis was relatively unimportant and unknowable; given the host of other
significant factors in the life of the child, it was impossible for any responsible professional to claim to be able to tease apart the supposed individual
disorder from the numerous factors that would have created the same behaviors in virtually any child who had been exposed to them. I no longer receive
referrals from this hospital.

It is interesting to speculate about what might have happened to the talking therapy professions if they had resisted the wave of medicalization that
hit the mental health scene several decades ago. Imagine if counselors,
psychologists, and social workers had refused to diagnose their clients, accept payment from health care insurers, and had steadfastly insisted that they
were talking, relational helpers and not health care providers. This is an
interesting historical thought experiment. On the one hand, refusal to participate in medicalization may have caused the talking therapy professions to
eventually become marginalized to the point of insignificance. However, it is
also possible that the refusal to participate in medicalization may have
caused these professions to thrive. In this regard, historical examples from
other professions might be instructive. Chiropractors and osteopaths, for instance, are well represented in modern health care. Both these professions
have unique ideological vantage points on health, which set them apart from
traditional medicine. However, osteopaths have been assimilated into allo-
pathic medicine, and the practices of modern D.O.s, at least in my observation, are largely indistinguishable from the practices of M.D.s. Alternatively,
chiropractors have generally remained true to their founding principles,
which has kept them from being folded into the traditional medical model.
Obviously, no one knows what would have happened to the talking therapy
professions if they had refused to become health care providers. However,

these historical examples of other professions provide some useful fodder for speculation.

Diagnostic and Statistical Manual

No critique or analysis of contemporary mental health culture would be complete without a critical examination of the Diagnostic and Statistical Manual (DSM). The DSM is the central nucleus around which mental health culture revolves, and it is emblematic of the medicalized focus on symptoms that characterizes modern practice. Despite its prominence, however, the DSM is riddled with foundational flaws, which are best understood in a historical context.

Throughout the history of their profession, psychiatrists have aspired to model their practices on standard medicine (Shorter, 1997). A diagnostic guide is a primary tool of medical practice. However, the first edition of the DSM, the primary diagnostic guide of the psychiatric profession, was not introduced until 1952, with the second edition appearing in 1968 (Mayes & Horwitz, 2005). These initial two editions of the DSM, rooted in psychoanalytic theory, were largely ignored by psychiatrists and other mental health professionals. However, the third edition, released in 1980, has virtually defined contemporary mental health culture.

During the 1970s Robert Sptizer, a psychiatrist, resolved to devote his career to the development of a third edition of the DSM (Spiegel, 2005). Not wanting to repeat the failures of the past manuals, Spitzer decided to change the ideological foundation of the new diagnostic guide to descriptive psychiatry, which is a nosological movement developed by Kraepelin at the turn of the twentieth century (Mayes & Horwitz, 2005; Shorter, 1997). Descriptive psychiatry is characterized by an exclusive focus on classifying disorders according to symptoms, without regard for etiological, theoretical, or treatment considerations (Hansen, 2005c). The descriptive psychiatric movement largely went underground in the twentieth century, due to the rise of psychoanalysis, which, with its dynamic, intrapsychic formulations, is essentially the ideological opposite of descriptive psychiatry (Shorter, 1997). However, Spitzer decided to revive descriptive psychiatry as an ideological foundation for the DSM-III (Mayes & Horwitz, 2005; Shorter, 1997; Spiegel, 2005)

It is certainly not self-evident that a purely symptom-based, descriptive model should be used for a psychiatric diagnostic manual. Indeed, there are numerous ways to classify human problems, including psychoanalytic (McWilliams, 2011), relational (Kaslow, 1993), and others. Descriptive psychiatry, then, is only one of many classificatory systems that could have been selected as the founding ideology for the DSM-III. The fact that contemporary mental health culture tends to focus almost exclusively on symptoms is largely a result of the descriptive psychiatric model that Spitzer chose for the

DSM-III, which, again, was a relatively arbitrary choice, given the host of alternatives.

That being said, there was some logic behind the selection of the descriptive psychiatric model as the basis for the DSM-III. When this new, third version of the DSM was being developed, the professional culture of mental health was highly parochial (Fancher, 1995). Practitioners and academics alike operated within particular ideological ecosystems, which were relatively independent and insulated from competing schools of thought. The psychoanalytic, behavioral, and humanistic communities, for instance, each had their own training centers, journals, and professional communities. Professional development essentially consisted of being indoctrinated into one of these schools of thought and remaining true to it throughout one's career (Fancher, 1995). Each community had radically different ways of describing client problems. For instance, psychoanalysts described clients according to intrapsychic principles, such as unconscious conflict. Behaviorists, alternatively, spoke exclusively in terms of observable behavior and measurable change.

This mix of ideological allegiances created difficulties when professionals from different schools of thought wanted to communicate with one another about clients. It was hoped that a descriptive psychiatric diagnostic guide would solve this problem. Everyone could presumably agree on the symptoms that a client displayed. A diagnostic manual based on symptoms alone, then, would facilitate communication between professionals from diverse ideological communities. Furthermore, a purely descriptive diagnostic guide might promote unified, objective research about mental health problems because all researchers would be investigating the same standardized groups of homogenous symptom clusters.

Spitzer, then, had a creative and compelling vision for the DSM-III that would presumably resolve some of the problems that had plagued psychiatric diagnostics for decades. Released in 1980, this new DSM, in contrast to the former editions, was wildly successful, in large part because it was an excellent ideological fit for the managed care and biological psychiatric movements that were ascendant at the time (Mayes & Horwitz, 2005). Far from being objective, though, this method of categorization based purely on symptoms gradually transformed into a dominant ideological orientation in its own right. Over the past three decades, this descriptive psychiatric vision has arguably overtaken mental health culture, thereby relegating psychological understandings of clients to a lowly ideological status (Hansen, 2005a).

This dominance of the DSM in mental health culture is, indeed, ironic, given a foundational, conceptual problem that is intrinsic to the psychiatric diagnostic enterprise. Specifically, as noted by Szasz (1961), a diagnostic system is nonsensical unless a stable, baseline definition of normality exists. If someone has a body temperature of 104 degrees Fahrenheit, for example, this person is ill, regardless of culture, location, or period of time when they are alive. This claim can be made because the consistent, normal baseline temperature of the human body is about 98 degrees. A temperature of 104 degrees represents a significant deviation from this norm. A phenomenon, therefore, can only be considered a disease or a disorder if it significantly deviates from an established baseline of normality (Hansen, 2003).

It follows, then, that psychiatric disorders, by definition, must represent deviations from some standard of normality; otherwise, they could not logically be defined as disorders. However, what is this standard of psychiatric normality? In this regard, it is useful to remember that psychiatrists were responsible for the greatest mass medical cure in history. This cure, which was instantaneous, impacted millions of people throughout the world at once. Specifically, in 1974, psychiatrists, by a narrow vote, decided that homosexuality should no longer be considered a mental illness (Shorter, 1997). Millions who had been afflicted with homosexuality were instantly cured.

When the societal definition of normal sexuality changed, so did psychiatric definitions of disordered sexuality. Unlike formal medical disorders, which are based on deviations from fixed, measurable, physiological baselines, psychiatric disorders are based on deviations from ever-fluctuating societal mores. It would be wonderful to be able to cure cancer or diabetes by vote. Although this obviously cannot be done, psychiatric disorders regularly change as a function of societal values and professional consensus. Lest the reader think that homosexuality is an unusual case, consider some other examples. During the time of slavery, drapetomania was a psychiatric diagnosis reserved for slaves who ran away from their masters (Whitaker, 2002). After all, went the disturbing reasoning of the time, primitive barbaric slaves who fled from the civilized existence that their benevolent masters provide must be mentally ill. As a contemporary example, "Dependent Personality Disorder" (American Psychiatric Association, 2000, p.721) is listed in the current version of the DSM. However, there is no independent personality disorder for those who show an unusual degree of independence from others. Independence is generally valued in our culture, while dependency is not (Fancher, 1995).

In addition to the foundational problem of not having fixed normative references, the DSM also suffers from a lack of basic psychometric properties (i.e., reliability and validity) that are essential for any categorical system to possess. As an example of the importance of reliability, imagine that you are about to weigh yourself on a scale. You step on and off this scale to obtain five readings of your weight within fifteen seconds. Suppose the scale indicated radical fluctuations, by hundreds of pounds, within this brief period of time. You would quickly conclude that the reading on the scale was meaningless because of this severe lack of consistency.

Consistency of measurement, which is referred to as *reliability* in psycho-metric terms, is a vital quality for a system of classification to possess. There is good evidence, though, that independent raters do not consistently rate the same clients with the same DSM diagnosis (Kirk & Kuchins, 1994), a situation that makes the DSM analogous to the inconsistent scale in the above example. Even if the argument is posed that highly trained experts in field trials generally rate clients consistently with the DSM criteria, consistent ratings almost certainly do not occur in practice. In my experience, it is common for practitioners to diagnose the same client differently, which is the reason that clients who have been in the mental health system for years often have a long list of diagnoses. Because of this lack of consistency (i.e., reli-ability), DSM diagnostics should arguably not be given any more credibility than the results of the hypothetical scale noted above.

In terms of validity, there is no evidence that the DSM categories repre-sent unified, underlying processes in the same way that symptoms of a sore throat and congested sinuses signify the presence of a virus (Fancher, 1995). Simply because the architects of the diagnostic manual grouped together various clusters of symptoms based on their observation that the symptoms in the clusters tend to cooccur or have certain commonalities, it does not necessarily follow that these symptom clusters represent unitary, underlying processes. To illustrate this point, I could create a category consisting of colorful phenomenon in the sky. Among other things, this category would include fireworks, rainbows, and volcanic eruptions. Despite the fact that I have clustered these phenomena together based on observed commonalities, it obviously does not mean that they emanate from the same source. Analo-gously, the symptom clusters in the DSM, which were grouped together by observation, do not necessarily represent unitary, underlying processes. In formal, psychometric terms, this means that the categories lack validity, which is a crippling problem for a manual of psychiatric disorders.

Despite these severe problems with the DSM, it is not unreasonable for the psychiatric profession to aspire to create a symptom-based diagnostic guide. Certain medications tend to help people who are afflicted with particu-lar symptom constellations. Theoretically, then, a manual that classifies these constellations, so that psychiatrists can match the proper medications with client problems, is a defensible idea. It is not evident, however, that this manual should include hundreds of different disorders. A few gross catego-ries (e.g., psychosis) based on medication responsiveness would seem to be all that is needed. Again, though, symptom-based diagnostics is arguably a tenable idea for a profession that has specific, effective treatments for partic-ular groups of symptoms.

However, simply because a symptom-based diagnostic guide may be use-ful for helping professionals who prescribe medications, it does not necessar-ily mean that the DSM has value for talking therapists. To determine whether a diagnostic manual based on symptom classification would be useful for counselors or psychotherapists, it is vital to know the factors that promote positive outcomes for clients who are seen by these professionals. If these outcome factors involve the prescriptive alignment of specialized treatments for particular disorders, then a descriptive psychiatric guide could conceivably be a useful tool for talking therapists. In this regard, there is abundant evidence that prescriptive matching of techniques to disorders is absolutely not an effective strategy for promoting positive outcomes in counseling or psychotherapy.

Wampold (2001), in an exhaustive, meta-analytic review of outcome research spanning several decades, compared the effectiveness of two psychotherapy paradigms: (1) the medical model, which highlights the role of prescriptive techniques for particular disorders; and (2) the contextual model, which emphasizes the therapeutic relationship and other factors that form the context of treatment. Not only was the contextual model the clear winner, but, as noted above, isolated techniques accounted for less than 1 percent of the variance in treatment outcomes. Clearly, the medical model of combating disorders by implementing specialized techniques is the wrong paradigm for talking therapists to adopt. This finding also means that a descriptive psychiatric manual is clinically useless for counselors and psychotherapists.

In fact, the DSM is probably worse than useless for talking therapists because the ideology that it promotes suppresses psychological understandings of clients. In this regard, I have conducted case conferences at various clinics, agencies, and hospitals for twenty years. At the beginning of my career, attendees often spontaneously talked about the internal conflicts, relationships, and defenses of their clientele. Currently, when I begin a new case discussion group, the attendees almost always talk in terms of diagnosis, medication, and treatment plans. I gradually counter this medicalized way of describing clients with psychological constructs, which are aimed at fleshing out the meaning systems and relational paradigms that their clients present. Depending on the composition of the group, sometimes my psychological descriptions are welcomed and other times they are resisted. Regardless, thinking in a medicalized way about clients is, unfortunately, the current norm, while conceptualizing cases according to the factors that have been proven to promote positive outcomes, such as the therapeutic relationship, meaning systems, and contextual elements of treatment, is rapidly becoming a lost art.

DISCUSSION

Mental health culture does not advance in a stepwise, progressive fashion. Using the metaphor of a pendulum, I have argued that ideological changes can be understood as regular historical swings, which have occurred over the past several centuries, between biological and psychosocial visions of emotional and behavioral problems. When one of these visions is dominant, the other is suppressed. Contemporary mental health culture is characterized by a biological, medicalized view of mental health problems, which has relegated conceptualizations of clients based on internal conflicts, relationships, and meaning systems to a lowly ideological status.

Rather than resisting this cultural trend, talking therapists have, in large part, eagerly carved out a role as ancillary health care providers in the mental health marketplace. This identification with the medical model has certainly served to increase the professional and economic status of counselors and psychotherapists. However, there is abundant and consistent evidence that the culturally suppressed relational, contextual model is a vastly superior paradigm for promoting positive client outcomes than the prescriptive, technical model that is currently in vogue.

Operating within this technocratic, medicalized mental health culture can create tremendous conflicts for practitioners who want to make a living using treatment approaches that are nuanced, relational, and based on well-established principles of psychology. Third party payers typically demand that psychotherapists and counselors document their work in the technical, reductionist language of diagnosis, symptoms, treatment plans, and measurable objectives. Consider the absurdity of this demand. In the hundred or so years since talking therapy was invented, no researcher or theorist has ever suggested that clients can best be helped by generating a descriptive, psychiatric diagnosis, breaking this diagnosis down into discrete symptoms, and then developing systematic, measurable plans to decrease each isolated problem. Yet, this is the model talking therapists must employ to receive insurance payment.

I do not blame the insurance companies for this situation, at least not entirely. Psychotherapists and counselors enthusiastically fought for the right to bill third party payers when managed care first emerged. Indeed, these professionals continue to mount legislative battles to be regarded as legitimate, health care providers who have a right to insurance reimbursement. Talking therapists made (and continue to make) their medical bed and resent having to lie in it. This sentiment, of course, is of little consolation to therapists who sincerely struggle to help their clients with methods that are the polar opposite of the absurdly reductionistic demands of third party payers.

This conflict, between doing right by clients and getting paid, casts a dark shadow over the professional lives of psychotherapists and counselors. There are various resolutions to this conflict. Some, for example, seem to forget everything they learned in graduate school about effective helping and completely identify with a managed care model. Others refuse to accept third party payments, establish private practices, and charge clients directly for services. Neither of these resolutions is a workable option for most, a situation that leaves many talking therapists feeling anxious, guilty, and angry about the conditions of their work.

As a practitioner who operates in multiple realms that are driven by third-party reimbursement, I have developed my own resolutions to this conflict. First, I continually try to keep client work and insurance demands strictly separate in my mind. Clinical work is about helping clients, and insurance demands, even though they may be superficially framed in quasi clinical terms, are exclusively about getting paid. These realms should not be intermixed or confused. Second, in terms of documentation, I conceptualize talking therapists and third party payers as different linguistic communities (Hansen, 2010a). Counselors and psychotherapists describe their work with professional language, such as transference, conflict, cognitive reframing, paradoxical intervention, and so on. Certain language systems have become prominent in the talking therapy professions because they are well suited for the work of helping clients. Alternatively, the language of third party payers, such as treatment plans and objectives, is suitable for micromanagement and cost containment, strategies that are designed to facilitate the financial success of insurance companies.

There is no correct way, above all others, to describe the helping encounter. Indeed, there are a potentially infinite number of language systems, such as sociological, poetic, and neurochemical, that could be used to meaningfully describe the act of one person attempting to help another through conversational means. Talking therapists just happen to use language systems to describe professional helping that are different from the powerful, dominant language system that is used by third party payers.

Given this conceptualization, I view documentation as an act of translation. When I document in terms of goals and objectives, for instance, I am simply providing my best translation of my professional descriptions into the language of the dominant linguistic community. The same would be true if I were to visit France, for example. I would translate my usual ways of describing the world into French, not be upset that France had not changed its official language to English. Of course, some important elements of what I intend to communicate might be lost in translation, but this is the price that is always paid for translating one language to another. This linguistic view of the documentation process helps me to report my work to third party payers, in their language, without feeling any guilt or resentment. I will let the reader decide whether I have discovered a workable conceptualization or have simply created an elaborate rationalization for being dishonest. I have yet to decide.

In addition to work-based conflicts with third party payers, the values endorsed by traditional therapists are often profoundly at odds with the values of the larger culture. The notions that money can buy happiness, having a wide range of people who know you can substitute for intimate relationships, and that direct, immediate action is always preferable to self-reflection, for example, are values that are generally endorsed in contemporary culture but rejected by traditional talking therapists (McWilliams, 2005). This makes traditional psychotherapeutic practice a countercultural activity (Hansen, 2010b). In my experience, the benefit of this countercultural position is that clients may have never considered the values that their therapists advocate. In this regard, I have often had the experience of offering a perspective to a client that seemed very ordinary and commonsensical to me, but was completely novel and even revelatory to the client. Of course, while some find countercultural sensibilities refreshing and insightful, others find them odd and unbearably discordant with their usual ways of being. Certain clients, for example, may drop out of treatment because they want quick, expert fixes, not a relational forum for self-reflection that is designed to bring about meaningful, hard won, and lasting change. There is certainly a downside, then, to being a traditional, countercultural psychotherapist.

In my experience, universities and other institutions that train talking therapists have gradually acquiesced to the technocratic values of the larger culture. Training to become a psychotherapist or counselor has become increasingly technical and medicalized over the past two decades (Hansen, 2003). Contemporary curricula typically include topics, such as the DSM, psychopharmacology, and symptom-based treatment planning, which are completely irrelevant to the mechanisms of change in the therapeutic encounter. Of course, knowledge about some of these topics is essential for practitioners to navigate the contemporary professional terrain. Offering this content as freestanding courses or as the bulk of a graduate, curriculum, however, symbolically sends the erroneous message that technical, psychiatric information is vitally important to the act of counseling (Hansen, 2003).

This emphasis on technical, medicalized training has also contributed to the ostracism of traditional therapeutic ideologies from the academy. Freudian theory, for instance, is often dismissed as the bizarre ramblings of a sexually obsessed man who analyzed his own cocaine-induced dreams. Representatives from research-based academic culture would like to be viewed as respectable scientists, not as purveyors of outdated, psychoanalytic fairy tales. In my view, though, psychoanalytic insights are vitally important for all budding therapists to learn. Underneath the psychosexual veneer of his theory, Freud essentially postulated that certain thoughts and experiences can be so shameful, painful, traumatic, and guilt inducing that people actively try to forget them. Sometimes, however, what was forgotten can come back to haunt us. To alleviate psychological suffering, psychotherapists should gently help clients to be honest with themselves and face the inner pain that they have desperately tried to disavow. Far from being bizarre, these core psychoanalytic principles are profound and commonsensical (Strenger, 1991).

Ironically, my view of modern psychotherapeutic training has probably been shaped more by my experiences as a consultant than by my university position. For instance, at a local clinic where I consult, I often supervise students during their graduate internship training. On one occasion, two new members, who were from the same school, joined my supervisory group. The DSM happened to be the topic of conversation on their inaugural visit to the group. I gave my usual speech to the attendees, saying that the DSM was useful for getting paid, but virtually useless, and even harmful, for the work of talking therapists. These two interns later told me that, upon hearing my attitude about the DSM, they subsequently informed their internship professor that they would probably have to complete their training at another site because they did not have faith in my professional competence. Their reaction was completely understandable. These students had been required to take three DSM courses in their master's curriculum. They could not understand how I could offhandedly dismiss a core part of their training, which, they were told, was vitally important to their work as counselors. Fortunately, they stayed at the site, came to appreciate my view of the therapeutic process, and we all laugh about this story now.

On another occasion, I served as the individual supervisor for a doctoral intern who had an extraordinary, natural talent for establishing therapeutic relationships. Unfortunately, her training had caused her to severely devalue this ability, and she usually spent her sessions with clients internally obsessing about the type of research, techniques, or theories that she should employ to combat particular symptoms. In an effort to undo the damaging impact of her education, I asked her to imagine, when in session with a client, that she was listening to a friend who had come over to her house in a state of distress. They were sitting on her living room couch together with a pot of coffee brewing in the background. I was confident that she knew enough about professional boundaries to get the gist of my metaphor without taking the friend analogy to an unhelpful extreme. This image helped her to activate the deeply attentive, relational side of herself, and to mentally leave the books at school. From these, and other, experiences, I believe that contemporary training to become a talking therapist often serves to suppress the talents of those who have natural abilities to do the work.

Fortunately, in the midst of this technocratic mental health culture, certain humanistic trends are starting to become influential. For example, I have argued that postmodernism, a philosophical movement that emphasizes human meaning construction, is the new humanism for our age (Hansen, 2012b). Narrative forms of therapies (e.g., deShazer, 1985; White & Epston, 1990) and qualitative research (Berg, 2004), both of which emphasize locally constructed truths, are postmodernist movements that have begun to shape the contemporary Zeitgeist (Hansen, 2010a). Furthermore, the concepts of human potential and happiness are beginning to come into vogue again with the rise of the wellness movement (Myers & Sweeney, 2005). Whether these strands of humanism can successfully band together to slay the medical Goliath is anyone's guess. Whatever ideological twists and turns the culture takes in the next decade, however, there can be no doubt that we live in interesting times.

Knowing the history and current state of mental health culture has been extraordinarily valuable to me as a professor and practitioner. Like philosophy, historical knowledge can help people stand outside of their current culture and view it from a critical perspective. For instance, I no longer take treatment fads very seriously because I know that mental health history is characterized by the continual introduction of flashy treatments, which are idealized for a short period of time and then abandoned for something shiny and new. I hope that this historical introduction has helped the reader to think critically about mental health culture. At the very least, it should provide a basis for understanding and critiquing the ideas that I present in the remainder of this book.

Chapter Two

Introduction to Philosophical Questions

As noted in the previous chapter, the helping professions have become highly medicalized over the past several decades (Chodoff, 2002; Hansen, 2005a; Shorter, 1997; Szasz, 2007b; Wampold, 2001). Students learn specialized techniques to help clients with particular problems. Professionals regularly diagnose their clients and provide treatments based on those diagnoses. Prescriptive, technical training and practice has become the norm, while deeper professional reflection has largely fallen by the wayside (Hansen, 2003; 2009a).

Many vital questions have been suppressed by this technical emphasis in contemporary mental health culture. What does it mean to help someone? Is getting rid of the symptoms helping, or should professionals attempt to change the psychological constitution of their clients? How do the values of the larger culture influence the helping professions? Can counselors ever view their clients objectively, or is there always a subjective component to professional decision making? These are only a few examples of important, philosophical questions that are no longer regularly considered by the helping industry.

However, why ask philosophical questions? After all, philosophers are often caricatured as ivory tower navel-gazers who formulate unanswerable questions and proceed to endlessly debate possible answers. Counselors seek to help people who are in a state of psychological distress. What could a philosopher possibly offer that would help a counselor with a depressed client, for instance? Philosophers have the luxury of asking whether someone should be allowed to take their own life, but helping professionals have no choice but to stop a client from committing suicide. Philosophical questioning is for armchair theoreticians, not professionals who actually work for a living.

From this critical vantage point, it does not seem as if there would ever be a reason for counselors to reflect on philosophical questions. Perhaps, then, counseling and philosophy are housed in separate university departments precisely because one discipline has nothing to do with the other. I suspect that many helping professionals would endorse this separatist point of view, particularly in contemporary mental health culture, which tends to idealize the technical and pragmatic components of helping while minimizing the role of reflective questioning and deeper understandings of the counseling relationship.

I am convinced, however, that there are compelling reasons to ask philosophical questions about counseling practice. Indeed, it is particularly important to engage in reflective questioning at this point in mental health history precisely because deeper questions have been suppressed by the contemporary Zeitgeist. I offer four fundamental reasons that regular philosophical reflection should be a vital component of counseling training and practice.

First, philosophical inquiry can bring about great change. Philosophers have been unfairly characterized as professionals who are incapable of making contributions to human betterment. Certainly, not every philosophical idea has practical implications, just as the ideas in most fields do not translate into revolutionary advances. However, even a casual glance back at the past few millennia will reveal the extraordinary contributions of philosophers.

The ancient Greeks, such as Plato, Aristotle, and Socrates, for instance, made revolutionary advances in the areas of education, government, and methods of inquiry that forever changed the course of human history (Tarnas, 1991). Enlightenment philosophers were responsible for formulating ideals, such as democracy, individualism, and reason, which became the bedrock of Western society (Hicks, 2004). Contemporarily, as medical advances often outpace our ability to morally digest them, bioethicists help us to comprehend the deeper implications of stem-cell research and human cloning. We should be forever grateful to the great thinkers of human history who were not afraid to ask the difficult, important questions and who had the courage to challenge the conventional wisdom of their times.

Indeed, accepted practices are never altered unless someone comes along and questions them. The only route to change and progress is to think differently, to challenge, persuade, oppose, and offer new ideas. In this way, many courageous acts surely started with basic philosophical questions. Rosa Parks' refusal to give up her seat on the bus, for instance, must have been preceded by a nagging internal question: Should people be treated differently on the basis of race? Arguably, admirable acts of defiance throughout human history have their origin in the willingness of people to ask the difficult, deep questions that philosophers regularly encourage us to contemplate.

Like the larger culture, the helping professions can only change and evolve if people are willing to consider fundamental questions. Sadly, philosophical inquiry has been largely dismissed as irrelevant in our contemporary, technocratic mental health culture. History teaches us, though, that human progress only occurs when foundational questions are asked and the answers are vigorously pursued. This is an important reason that philosophical inquiry should be part of the training and the ongoing professional life of all helping professionals.

Second, philosophical questions help to illuminate the assumptions behind current practices. For instance, during the mid-century heyday of psychiatric hegemony, Szasz (1961) offered his unsettling conclusion that mental illness was a myth. Szasz used the careful reasoning, analysis, and unconventional thinking that is often employed by philosophers to critically examine the assumptions that were at the heart of psychiatric practice. His initial philosophical questions led to revolutionary changes in mental health practices, including deinstitutionalization and the anti-psychiatry movement (Schaler, 2004).

As another example, the helping professions evolved for decades with an unexamined assumption: problems reside in individuals (Fowers & Richardson, 1996). All founding theoretical orientations, from psychoanalysis to behaviorism to humanism, were structured by this assumption. This led practitioners to diagnose individuals, conduct treatment with individuals, and judge outcomes by the degree to which individuals changed. However, the family systems (e.g., Minuchin, 1974) and social constructionist (Gergen, 1999) movements helped to reveal and critique this implicit assumption. Perhaps problems reside in collections of people, not individuals. Maybe the unit of treatment concern should not be individuals, but systems. Without a penetrating analysis of the assumptions behind individual therapy, these movements, and the associated treatment paradigms, would have never been launched.

In this regard, psychological theories always proceed from certain bedrock assumptions. These assumptions must be understood in order to fully appreciate and comprehend the theories. Psychoanalytic theory, for instance, initially presumed that clinicians could arrive at objective conclusions about their clients (Gill, 1994). Except in the case of interference from countertransference (Freud, 1910/1957), the early psychoanalysts were confident that psychoanalytic training provided them with the necessary background to view their clients without bias. In the past three decades, however, this assumption has been critiqued (e.g., Hoffman, 1998). Many modern psychoanalytic practitioners do not endorse the assumption that therapists can be objective. The philosophical critique of this objectivity hypothesis has led to innovative advances in psychoanalytic practice (e.g., Stolorow, Brandchaft & Atwood, 1995).

Ideologies and practices are always embedded in a network of assumptions, which are determined by the current culture. Without systematic philosophical questioning, these assumptions would be accepted at face value. Philosophical questioning provides a special lens that helps us see beyond practices to the foundational ideas that support them. If it were not for the logical tools that philosophy provides, we would be prisoners of our times, thereby unable to consider the impact of power, culture, and history on currently fashionable ideas.

Third, philosophical questioning is the best defense against the theoretical dogmatism that has long plagued the mental health professions. Historically, helping professionals were often trained to have allegiance to a particular theory (Fancher, 1995). Although the situation is not as bad today as it was thirty years ago, theoretical dogmatism continues to bedevil the mental health professions. For instance, some practitioners are strict cognitive-behaviorists, while others have allegiance to humanism. When one devotes his or her training to mastering a particular orientation to treatment, it can be very difficult to adopt insights from competing orientations. Theories are often insulated by ideological walls, which make competing theories seem superficial or nonsensical (Fancher, 1995; Hansen, 2002).

For example, to a traditional psychoanalyst, the idea of changing a client's thinking through cognitive-behavioral methods is a simplistic and superficial approach to treatment that could not possibly have any lasting impact. Alternatively, to the cognitive-behaviorist, the psychoanalyst is wasting his or her time by pursuing a mythical unconscious that has no bearing on the problems with which clients struggle. If one has spent years mastering the theory and treatment approach of a particular orientation, it can be incredibly difficult to assimilate ideas from competing theories because these ideas will almost always be counter to the core assumptions of the favored theory.

Philosophical questioning helps to highlight the things we do not know, the often shaky foundation upon which definitive theoretical assertions are made, and the vast areas of gray in a field that can never be accurately characterized as black and white. Whenever someone makes a certain claim in the helping professions, a few probing questions is usually all that it takes to reveal the actual lack of certainty that the claim represents. Therefore, philosophical questioning promotes critical thinking, combats dogmatism, and encourages flexibility in practice and theorizing.

Fourth, immersion in philosophical ideas can give practitioners an intellectual respite from the difficult work of counseling clients. Helping people find a way out of their psychological pain is an incredibly draining way to make a living. Practitioners often see one hopeless, addicted, and traumatized individual after another. When clients get better, they are discharged and replaced with fresh sufferers, thereby continually exposing therapists to the raw, painful side of life.

Years of formal education are required to become a therapist. Those who eventually enter the helping professions, then, often enjoy ideas and academic topics. In this regard, philosophical questioning can provide professionals with a welcome intellectual reprieve from the onslaught of human pain to which they are continually exposed. For instance, rather than empathize with a client's history of trauma, it might be a welcome break for a practitioner to contemplate the meaning of trauma, what constitutes a trauma, and whether a trauma should be defined according to some objective scale or the subjective meaning system of individuals.

Some might consider this function of philosophical questioning as avoidance or a defense. Perhaps they would be right, but I am not sure that this is a bad thing. As part of professional self-care, practitioners need a way to rejuvenate their professional interests while taking a break from the emotional pressure-cooker of the therapy office. Contemplating deep questions can help keep interest in the field alive while providing an intellectual vacation from the continual exposure to psychological pain that is a routine part of the day in the life of a therapist.

MY STORY

I present the ideas in this book in the context of my personal intellectual struggles. There are three reasons that I have chosen this format rather than simply presenting the ideas alone. First, ideas, of course, always originate from an experiencing human being. By positioning the intellectual material in this book within my personal experiences, I hope that this will give the material a richness, nuance, and meaning that would not be available without the autobiographical context. Second, I have always admired clinical writers, such as Yalom (1989), Kottler (2010), and McWilliams (2004), who disclose their feelings, struggles, self-doubts, and conflicts when they describe their work with clients. In contrast to the technical, experientially barren guides that dominate the literary canon of the helping professions, there is a refreshing honesty and realness to the deeply relational accounts of counseling and psychotherapy that these authors provide. In this book, I have attempted to extend this relational, self-disclosure style of writing into the realm of ideas. Anyone who finds certain ideas intrinsically fascinating is probably familiar with the quasi-relational experiences that are often elicited by intellectual immersion. The thrill of discovery; unbridled enthusiasm about a novel theory; conflicts about facing conceptual limitations; grief over the recognition that the initial idealization was unwarranted; and struggles about whether to continue the ideological relationship in the face of logical inconsistencies are all a part of the highs and lows of courting ideas. Rather than suppress these experiences, I wanted to highlight them to add authenticity, meaning, and richness to the material, akin to the way that clinical writers whom I admire enrich their vignettes by disclosing the personal experiences that were elicited by the helping encounter. Third, I anticipate this book will be read primarily by professionals who spend their days getting to know the lives of their clients. Taking a reader-centric approach, then, means that I should provide readers with a literary experience that they find familiar, engaging, and intriguing—an optimal balance between a theoretical textbook and the *National Enquirer*. I present a rough overview of my intellectual journey below.

I have always been fascinated by subjectivity, consciousness, and individual differences. Therefore, when I applied to graduate programs in psychology, I deliberately chose a doctoral program that had a psychoanalytic orientation, because this orientation seemed to have the most promise to satisfy my intellectual yearnings. After immersing myself in psychoanalytic thought and practice for six years, I graduated and eventually took a job as a staff psychologist in an inpatient psychiatric hospital.

At first, I really enjoyed the work. I felt fortunate to have a full-time, salaried position in a mental health economy where such positions were increasingly becoming a rarity. The job also allowed me to work with schizophrenics, a population in which I always had a strong interest. However, as the months and years went by, I became increasingly dissatisfied with my job.

Cognitive-behavioral and psychopharmacological interventions were the treatment of choice in the early 1990s when I first started the job. Psychoanalytic interventions were considered passé at best, and bizarre and irrelevant at worst, particularly when applied to schizophrenia. Also, there was no room for advancement at the hospital. Indeed, there was even talk that full-time staff psychologists would be replaced by contractual consultants. Just two years after I had earned my doctorate degree, I was in a state of career crisis. I had been young and academically sheltered during my years at the university. I never anticipated that I might not make a living as a full-time inpatient psychologist using psychoanalytic methods on inpatient schizophrenic patients. I now look back and laugh at my naiveté.

My anxiety about my career had been bothering me for nearly a year when a possible solution finally occurred to me: I could become a professor. Although I had taught part-time for several years at local universities while working at the hospital, I had never considered a full-time academic position. However, when I began to reflect on the aspects of my work that I found most fulfilling, I concluded that I enjoyed two aspects of my job the most: teaching and research. In my hospital position, I taught the principles of psychotherapy to a variety of professionals, including medical students, social workers, and psychologists. I also initiated and oversaw a research study, which was eventually published. Based on my reflective observation that I was acting like a professor by progressively engaging in teaching and research, I concluded that I must want to be a professor.

Interestingly, up to that point, I had never considered a career in academia. Because my doctoral degree was in clinical psychology, I had not considered a career outside of clinical work. This is the only reason I can think of that the relatively obvious conclusion that I should become a professor did not occur to me earlier in my career. From that point forward, I decided that I, not the title of my degree, would determine my career.

When I thought about where I would like to be a professor, I immediately concluded that the Department of Counseling at Oakland University would be my first choice. I had taught as a part-timer at Oakland for the previous couple of years. I enjoyed the students and the unique contribution I made as a psychologist in a counseling department. Fortunately, just when I concluded that I wanted to become a professor at Oakland, a one-year visiting position became available in the department. When I was offered the job, I asked my then very pregnant wife if she would mind if I left the hospital job for a one-year position that might not be renewed (this was immediately after we had just bought our first house). To this day I thank her for saying "go for it."

In the fall of 1995 I began as a visiting assistant professor. Within the first week, I knew that I had found the right job for me. I loved the teaching and the professional autonomy that was part of professorial life. After the year was up, I successfully competed for a tenure-track position. I began as a tenure-track assistant professor in the fall of 1996.

Entering professorial life required me to undergo the usual adjustments and transformations that are the norm for new faculty. However, because of my training as a psychoanalytic psychologist, I also had the additional challenge of entering a culture of helping that was structured along entirely different lines than the culture of my training. Specifically, the theoretical orientation that I had idealized and spent years studying was generally of little importance to members of the counseling profession, who tended to identify with a humanistic approach to helping. Moreover, it quickly became apparent to me that counselors did an excellent job of helping clients without psychoanalytic principles, an observation that only served to increase my level of internal dissonance.

There are potentially many ways that I could have responded to this dissonance. For example, I could have given up my familiar orientation and fully embraced humanism or become defensively locked into psychoanalytic thought. Instead of these resolutions, I chose to amplify, rather than suppress, my conflict and utilize it as a launching pad for scholarly inquiry. Consequently, my scholarly focus became the theoretical integration of diverse counseling orientations.

My initial, rough attempts at theoretical integration were aimed at importing psychoanalytic concepts into humanistic thought, which is the general topic area of my early published articles. Notably, during this period, another interest, which was also a natural outgrowth of my intellectual struggles, began to emerge: critiques of contemporary mental health culture.

With regard to contemporary mental health culture, one common theoretical feature of both humanism and psychoanalysis is the high regard that these orientations have for subjectivity and the counseling relationship. It was alarming to me, then, that mental health culture seemed to be rapidly abandoning these traditional values and trading them for an emphasis on descriptive diagnostics, and other varieties of medicalization, that are suppressive to human subjectivity. Therefore, one focus of my scholarship has been to challenge the dominant medical model and call for a renewed emphasis on the counseling relationship and subjective meaning systems.

To return to my primary area of scholarship, my early attempts at theoretical integration were, ultimately, dissatisfying to me. I concluded that integration, on a grand scale, could never be achieved by simply importing discrete techniques or concepts from one theoretical camp to another. During the phase that grew out of this dissatisfaction, I attempted more theoretically-based integrations to identify conceptual commonalities of humanism and psychoanalysis that could be exploited for the purpose of grand unification. Ultimately, I became frustrated at the lack of fit between these orientations.

Out of this frustration, I began to consider Audre Lordes' (1984) brilliant and provocative insight that "the master's tools will never dismantle the master's house" (p. 11). Of course, she never intended this insight to be applied to something as banal as my scholarly interests, but I thought that her thinking might help me out of my jam. As applied to my interests, I took Lordes' insight to mean that my concerns about counseling could only be accomplished by viewing these concerns from the perspective of another discipline. Philosophy, because it is dedicated to exploring basic and fundamental questions, seemed like a good candidate for this other discipline. I also had a strong academic foundation and interest in philosophy.

My forays into philosophy led me straight to the postmodernist movement, which, at the time, was just beginning to have an influence on counseling theorizing. Postmodernist thought was incredibly illuminating to me and quickly became a core part of my intellectual foundation. During this phase, I began to entertain new questions in the realms of subjectivity, intersubjectivity, and epistemology. However, postmodernist thought, while it provided solutions, also had problems of its own, such as solipsism, relativism, and a penchant for nihilistic deconstructionism that did not suit my scholarly purposes. My dissatisfaction with formal postmodernism eventually led to neo-pragmatism, which is an offshoot of postmodernist thought that has assimilated the insights of the earlier pragmatist movement. I discuss each of these philosophical movements, and their conceptual implications for understanding the counseling relationship, later in the book.

To summarize my development as a scholar, I have attempted to answer a series of questions about theoretical integration, mental health culture, subjectivity, and epistemology from different ideological perspectives. When my intellectual conflicts about a particular perspective began to mount, I searched for alternative conceptual models that were more satisfying. It has been an incredibly rich and satisfying intellectual journey for me. I still cannot believe that I found a way to make a living by following my curiosities to wherever they take me.

Along the way, as is customary in academia, my progress as a scholar was reviewed by fellow professors and university administrators to assess my eligibility for promotion and tenure. Anyone who has prepared a dossier for academic review knows that it is a fairly dreadful process. Assembling and summarizing years of work, chasing down bits of documentation to prove that you have actually engaged in the tasks that you reference, and organizing the hundreds of pages according to inane and arbitrary administrative standards is anything but fun. For me, however, the task did have a positive and unexpected side effect: It caused me to reflect more deeply on my work.

This reflective process caused me to retrospectively narrate my scholarly journey in novel ways. One of the most meaningful ways that I came to think about my scholarly process is what I have called the "conference table metaphor." This metaphor, which I believe is a fairly accurate depiction of the experiential side of my scholarly process, goes something like this: There is a conference table in my head where intellectuals meet to talk. To earn a seat at the table, one must have formulated ideas that sent me on the equivalent of an intellectual LSD trip. Only thinkers who blew my mind, turned my world upside down, and whose ideas churned inside of me for at least a decade could earn a seat. Four people sit at the table: Sigmund Freud; Carl Rogers; Thomas Szasz; and Richard Rorty.

Sigmund Freud invented talking therapy and psychoanalysis. When I first encountered his writings, I was completely enthralled. Freud's rich, layered, and dynamic conceptualization of subjectivity and his bold, courageous presentation of controversial ideas made him a hero to me. The leader of the humanistic movement, Carl Rogers, changed the course of counseling and psychotherapy forever when he rejected the reductionism of psychoanalysis and behaviorism for a holistic appreciation of authentic, relational encounters. During the mid-twentieth century, Rogers (1957) propounded radical ideas that were consistently verified decades later, such as the importance of the therapeutic relationship and the relative unimportance of education to being a good therapist. Thomas Szasz, the ultimate intellectual rebel and only conference table participant whom I have had the honor to meet, was a psychiatrist who spent his career critiquing the ideological foundations of psychiatry. Szasz's arguments are highly compelling and challenge almost every element of conventional reasoning about mental health issues. I admire the first three conference table participants for their originality, intellectual courage, and the fact that they taught me to think in completely new ways. The fourth participant, Richard Rorty, however, changed my outlook about virtually everything. Rorty began his career as a conventional, analytic philosopher. However, he eventually developed a highly original synthesis of American pragmatism and European postmodernism to form neopragmatism, a philosophical movement that is reviewed later in this book. Rorty profoundly influenced my thinking and helped me to harmonize the cacophonous voices of the other conference table participants. The work of Freud, Rogers, Szasz, and especially Rorty form the bedrock of my intellectual frame of reference.

These four intellectuals get together for regular meetings in my mind. Although I have the greatest admiration for each of them, they seldom agree with each other. Fights sometimes break out, names are called, and peaceful resolutions are hard to find. At times, when the participants have been in a receptive mood, I have invited guest speakers to the conference. Notable guests have included Kenneth Gergen, Jane Flax, Jerome Frank, Bruce Wampold, William James, Irvin Yalom, Robert Fancher, Barbara Held, and Daniel Dennet. Rorty chairs all of the discussions, because, in my estimation, he is the most important unifying force in the group.

I play a relatively minor role in the meetings: I sit by the side of the table and take minutes. I record the points that are made by my four intellectual heroes during their discussions. Because I idealize each of them, I suffer from cognitive dissonance when they disagree. Therefore, when I note a rare flash of agreement, I try to capitalize on it by highlighting the agreement in the minutes. After the minutes have been recorded and organized, I submit them for publication.

As I began to think of my scholarly journey according to this conference table metaphor, new narrative layers of my inquiry process began to emerge. Specifically, it occurred to me that, over many years of conferencing, my four chatty geniuses had primarily argued about four questions: (1) What does it mean to know a client? (2) What makes counseling effective? (3) Are truths discovered or created in the counseling relationship? and (4) Should counselors abandon the idea of truth? The primary purpose of this book is to explore these questions.

To provide a brief preview of these questions, it is not obvious what it means to know someone. How do you know when you know someone? Does knowing a client entail thorough familiarity with the client's unconscious mental life, as Freud would argue, or are people fundamentally transparent? Indeed, can one person ever know another, or is each person forever locked into their own impenetrable psychological universe? This first question about knowing is related to the second about effectiveness. After all, knowing someone would seem to be a prerequisite to helping them. What makes counseling effective, though? Indeed, how should effectiveness be defined? Perhaps symptomatic relief should be the only goal of helping. On the other hand, maybe truly effective counseling should help clients resolve longstanding issues and rearrange the dynamics of their inner life. Perhaps symptomatic relief should only be considered a mere side effect of these deeper processes.

The third question about whether truths are discovered or created in the counseling relationship arises naturally from the first two questions. Suppose a counselor identifies a psychological or relational process and the client, who had previously been unaware of this process, acknowledges that the counselor is correct. Does this interaction mean that the counselor, by virtue of her or his expertise, had discovered something about the client, which had been their all along, that the client had missed? Or, alternatively, did the counselor and client progressively negotiate a storyline that felt experientially real to the client, but was not true in the sense of being a longstanding process that was discovered by the counselor? This third question hints at the role of truth in the counseling process, and the fourth question asks whether counselors should abandon truth altogether. Is truth the route to healing? What are the consequences of simply forgetting about the ideal of truth? If truth is abandoned, what might be a suitable replacement to guide the counseling process?

One chapter is devoted to each question. Each chapter begins with an overview of the question. Then, I discuss the personal and professional significance of the question. Next, I entertain possible answers. Last, I conclude each chapter with a discussion of the pertinent points and possible resolutions. I certainly hope that you enjoy the journey as much as I have.

Chapter Three

What Does it Mean to Know a Client?

At first glance, this may seem like a silly and trivial question. However, the more one thinks about the question, the more fleeting the answer becomes. We commonly speak of knowing someone. I know my departmental secretary, my wife, the person I met at a party last weekend, my children, and my mail carrier. If a skeptical questioner were to ask me how I knew that I know these people, I might respond that I have had conversations with each of them, and my knowledge about them is often verified by their responses to me. For instance, I know that my youngest child likes spicy food, and my oldest abhors it, because I have had multiple experiences and conversations with them that have verified these preferences. I know them.

My hypothetical questioner might continue to press me, though. Does the preference for a certain type of food really constitute knowing someone? If not, what would constitute a full knowing of another person? At what point could you finally proclaim that you know someone? In my defense, I might respond that I know people to different degrees. Knowing is a continuum, not a binary. However, my questioner's dissatisfaction with these responses might lead him or her to raise a whole new set of troubling problems about my claims to know other people.

For instance, my questioner might point out that for me to know someone it must mean that elements of the other person's experience are duplicated in my mind. For me to claim, for instance, that I know that my wife finds animal abuse incredibly troubling, it must mean the following: (a) In my wife's mind, there is a specific content related to feelings about animal abuse; and (b) this same content has been recreated and stored in my mind. If the two mental contents match, I can claim that I know my wife (at least with regard to this issue). To know someone, then, must mean that there is a match between certain contents of the mind of the person who is known and the knower. However, my questioner might wryly point out, there is no way to verify that certain contents of my mind accurately correspond to parallel contents of the mind of the person whom I claim to know. We cannot observe the contents of anyone's mind. How, then, can we be sure that this match exists?

I might respond that I know that this match exists because the people I claim to know verify some of the things that I know about them. If I were to approach my wife and ask her if she finds animal abuse troubling, she would say that she does. This, I might argue, is verification of the matching contents of our respective minds.

At this point, my persistent questioner might argue that all of my knowledge claims about other people are dependent upon the communicative vehicle of language. I would be forced to admit that my questioner is probably right about this. I know that my friend identifies with progressive political positions because he has told me so. I know that Thomas Edison was an extremely persistent inventor because I have read about him. I know that the editor does not like my latest article because he wrote me a rejection email saying so. Knowing would seem to be a language dependent phenomenon (Hansen, 2008).

In order for one person to know another, my questioner might argue, language must be an adequate vehicle for capturing and communicating human experience because knowing is always dependent upon language. In order for the contents of my mind to match certain elements of the mind of the person whom I claim to know, language must function according to the following communicative steps: (a) some sort of content exists in the other person's mind; (b) the other person translates this content into language, which is communicated to me; and (c) I receive the linguistic communication, interpret the language, and store the associated content in my mind.

However, there are multiple problems with assuming that these steps could ever work smoothly and accurately. Most importantly, rich layers of human experience are certainly lost when they are shoehorned into the "grunts and squeals" (Frederickson, 1999, p. 252) of language (Spence, 1982). Just like a cheap whistle cannot adequately convey the richness of a symphony, language is arguably a completely inadequate tool to convey the complex dimensions of human experience. Therefore, because knowing is a language dependent phenomenon, it seems absurd to presume that the contents of one person's mind can be accurately transmitted (with all the richness and webs of meanings that accompany even the simplest thoughts) to the mind of another person.

What it means to know a client, then, is not a simple question to answer. The challenges raised by my hypothetical questioner reveal a host of problems associated with the claim that one person can know another. Most people probably do not give these issues much thought. However, something

about my intellectual and emotional disposition made this issue very meaningful to me, even at an early age.

PERSONAL AND PROFESSIONAL
SIGNIFICANCE OF THE QUESTION

Since childhood, before I could articulate the experience, I have felt a strong,
underlying sense of isolation. I do not mean isolation in the conventional
sense of being alone. I have always had a good number of friends, supportive
family, and other people in my life with whom I have felt a close connection.
By isolation, I mean a deeply felt sense of fascination and distress that my
mind was completely separated from the minds of others. I have always felt
like I lived in my head. I was acutely aware that the rich interplay of thoughts
that I had while walking home from school, for instance, could never be
recreated and placed wholly in the mind of another person. No one could
ever fully understand me. I was alone.

   This sense of existential isolation has always been part of my experience,
although it has not always been fully conscious. I never experienced severe
distress about it, but it began to well up in my mind as I got older. I believe
that my sense of isolation was largely responsible (although I was not completely aware of it at the time) for my choice to become a psychology major
at college. While in high school, I had heard that psychologists had a number
of theories related to understanding the inner life of human beings. Perhaps, I
unconsciously reasoned, I might be able to solve the riddle of personal isolation by studying psychology.

   Psychology was a fascinating course of study for me. Of all the theorists I
read, though, Sigmund Freud was the one who appealed to me the most.
Reading his *Introductory Lectures* (Freud, 1916/1963) and the *Interpretation
of Dreams* (Freud, 1900/1953) was an awe-inspiring, life-changing experience. Unlike other theorists, Freud offered sophisticated maps of the mind. I
thought that I might be able to use his maps to find my way out of isolation.
Furthermore, Freud added a radical, intriguing, and frightening addendum to
my sense of isolation: not only was knowing others problematic, people were
not even capable of knowing themselves! Freud's map of the mind baited
me, but the idea of an unconscious reeled me in. I was hooked.

   I subsequently enrolled in a doctoral program in clinical psychology. I
purposefully chose a program that had a strong psychoanalytic orientation. I
spent six deeply satisfying years immersed in Freudian psychology and practice. Along the way, I developed an interest in schizophrenia.

   I retrospectively understand my interest in schizophrenia as emanating
from the same source as my interest in psychoanalysis. Both interests grew
out of my sense of isolation. I found talking with schizophrenics reassuring

because the isolated nature of their existence is often obvious. When an individual who suffers from schizophrenia makes a claim that no one else believes (that he is Jesus Christ, for instance) it is quite obvious that the schizophrenic person is alone in his experience. When we speak with people who generally share our beliefs, in contrast, it is not obvious that isolation is operative. For instance, if a colleague shares her frustration with me about an issue at the university, I nod my head, make an attempt to empathize with her concerns, and provide various signs that I have understood the nature of her frustration. We do not feel isolated because we had the sense that a true sharing of minds occurred during the interaction. What a lie! Schizophrenia, to me, was the boldest and most personally validating statement of the truth: We are always alone.

After graduation, I naively sought a job where I could put my two interests into practice by conducting psychoanalytic therapy with schizophrenics. It is hard to imagine worse career goals for a psychologist in the early 1990s when the medical model and cognitive behaviorism ruled the day. Remarkably, I landed a job in an inpatient psychiatric hospital where I could pursue my interests.

Although the work was satisfying on certain levels, I gradually grew tired with the hospital routine. After three years at the hospital, I accepted a professorial position in the Department of Counseling at Oakland University. As a new professor, I was expected to launch a program of scholarly inquiry. I eventually settled on an exploration of philosophical issues in counseling. In retrospect, it is easy for me to see that many of the issues that I explored in my writing emanated from the same sense of isolation that had structured virtually all of my career choices. Writing became a type of therapy for me, an intellectual, investigative way to unravel the knot of isolation that was stuck in the craw of my psyche.

Although the issue of knowing was personally important to me, it is also an important issue for all helping professionals to consider. At its core, the work of counseling or therapy involves an extended conversation between people. In individual counseling, the client comes to the counselor for relief from psychological distress. The counselor attempts to orchestrate ongoing conversations in a way that will help the client overcome the distress. Presumably, regardless of theoretical orientation, the counselor must come to know clients in order to help them.

But, how does this process of knowing work, particularly in light of the critique presented in the first part of this chapter? Is knowing a prerequisite for helping? What is the relevant information about clients that counselors should know? How can counselors be sure that their knowledge about clients is accurate? These are difficult questions, but, in some ways, the entire enterprise of helping depends upon the answers.

Unfortunately, most psychological theorists do not provide us with much help. Most of the great theoretical architects of the helping professions were not concerned about formal philosophical questions. However, it is often possible to detect their implicit assumptions about knowing from reading their work.

WHAT DOES IT MEAN TO KNOW A CLIENT?

In my estimation, the most important theorists to plumb the depths of subjectivity were Sigmund Freud and Carl Rogers. Therefore, any consideration of knowing in the helping professions must draw from their work.

Freud and Psychoanalysis

One of the great tragedies of modern mental health culture is that Freudian ideas are dismissed as the bizarre, antiquated ramblings of a sexually obsessed man whose treatment methods were interminable and ineffective. Contemporary textbooks in psychological theories typically devote only a few paragraphs to Freud, usually citing his most ridiculous sounding concepts, such as castration anxiety and penis envy. He is often treated like an odd museum piece, a reminder of what the helping professions used to be like before we moved on to modern, effective treatments, such as cognitive behavioral approaches.

This disregard of Freud is a great disservice to modern students and trainees because Freud had some of the most profound ideas in the history of the helping professions. Indeed, psychoanalytic concepts have arguably had a powerful influence on all modern theories of mental health practice. Because his intellectual temperament was not suited to philosophical speculation, Freud did not address esoteric, philosophical issues about knowing (Gay, 1988). His implicit assumptions about knowing, though, can be inferred from his work. These assumptions can only be understood in the context of the historical and theoretical development of psychoanalytic thought.

Freud was a Viennese neurologist. Turn-of-the-century outpatient neurology was very different from modern neurological practice. Freud and his colleagues treated patients who were diagnosed with hysteria, which is what the people of that time called odd symptoms that had no obvious connection to physical impairment or that even outright contradicted what was then known about medicine (Gay, 1988). For instance, glove paralysis, a condition that involved paralysis of the hand when the arm was fully functional, was known at the time to be a physical impossibility (McWilliams, 1999). Therefore, hysterical conditions, Freud reasoned, must have some kind of psychological causation.

Freud eventually became intrigued by the problems that were presented to him in his neurological practice. He tried many treatment methods, including hypnosis. He finally settled on a core set of ideas and practices that would shape the future of the helping professions.

Although many schools of psychoanalytic thought eventually emerged, the central assumption of psychoanalysis is that mental health problems are caused by unconscious conflict (Gabbard, 2010). Freud initially proposed that the unconscious contained repressed sexual fantasies from childhood (Gay, 1988). When these fantasies are activated in adulthood, they begin to emerge and express themselves in disguised, derivative form as symptoms. This conceptualization of symptoms made sense out of conditions like glove paralysis, which Freud theorized was a derivative, symptomatic expression of an unconscious wish to masturbate along with the accompanying inhibitions against doing so (McWilliams, 1999).

Once the unconscious was established as the centerpiece of psychoanalytic theory, Freud had to find a way to access the unconscious mental life of his patients. Knowing someone else's unconscious would seem to be a difficult, if not impossible, task. After all, if a person, by definition, cannot access his or her own unconscious, how can an outsider, like Freud, gain access to it? The method that he finally settled upon to come to know the unconscious of his patients was free association, a method which was ideologically derived from the principle of psychic determinism (Gabbard, 2010).

As a neurologist, Freud knew that neurons were interconnected throughout the body. Particular neuronal firings regularly triggered other neurons to fire. Neurons, then, were subject to the same deterministic, cause and effect laws that governed the rest of the physical world. Like all physical reality, there were no random events in the brain or nervous system. If a neuron fires, for instance, there must have been a preceding event, just like if a ball rolls, something must have pushed it. Ultimately, Freud reasoned, mental life must also be beholden to these deterministic laws because the contents of the mind emanate from a physical foundation (i.e., neurons and the brain). Therefore, if someone is encouraged to speak freely and spontaneously about the contents of their mind, whatever the person says must be interconnected, even if, on the surface, the various thoughts seem to have nothing to do with each other. The idea that the psyche was just as determined as the physical world thus gave rise to the technique of free association (Eagle, 2011).

Freud, then, encouraged his patients to lie on a couch and spontaneously report whatever was on their mind without editing the contents (i.e., free association) while he sat behind them, out of their field of vision. Going on the assumption of psychic determinism (i.e., that all of his patient's thoughts were tightly determined even if they seemed random), Freud focused on inferring the contents of the unconscious from interconnections and slips of the tongue in his patient's free associations. For instance, if a patient talked about her husband and then spontaneously began talking about her father, Freud assumed, based on the principle of psychic determinism, that there must be some connection between husband and father in the patient's unconscious. With the technique of free association, and the concepts of psychic determinism and the unconscious, Freud had a workable set of tools to help his patients. He could infer the unconscious determinants of the free associations and interpret those determinants to his patients, thereby making them aware of the actual, hidden forces that were driving their symptoms. Through this awareness, patients could free themselves from developmentally-based conflicts that were no longer relevant to their current life. However, one seemingly insurmountable problem emerged: Freud's patients began to talk about him.

As Freud quietly sat behind the couch, his patients often free associated to their fantasies about him, perhaps thinking that he was secretly angry with them, trying to seduce them, or bored by their talk. At first, Freud was discouraged by this development. After all, how was he to help patients if they talked about their therapist instead of their issues? Eventually, however, Freud reasoned that when his patients talked about him, it must represent a reliving (i.e., transferring) of some older conflict that was brought into the present therapeutic situation. The concept of transference was born (Storr, 1989).

Transference is a like a psychological time machine. As an adult, it is impossible, to go back in time and readdress childhood conflicts. With transference, however, developmentally-based conflicts emerge with full emotional intensity in the therapy situation, thereby making them available to be worked through in the present (Gabbard, 2010). Transference logically led Freud to formulate the parallel concept of countertransference, which is the transference of the therapist to the patient (Freud, 1910/1957). At the time Freud conceived of countertransference, he thought that it was a negative force that would cause therapists to distort the psychoanalytic process by superimposing their own issues onto the patient. This led Freud to mandate that all psychoanalytic trainees undergo psychoanalytic treatment, so that countertransference issues would be worked through and resolved before the trainee became a full-fledged psychoanalyst (Gabbard, Litowitz & Williams, 2012).

It is important to understand basic psychoanalytic concepts, such as psychic determinism and transference, to appreciate Freud's implicit ideas about what it means to know a client. The most fertile ground for inferring Freud's conceptualizations about client knowledge are probably his papers on techniques, which grew out of his foundational assumptions about the psychoanalytic process. These techniques were arguably designed to ensure objectivity (Gabbard, 2005).

For instance, Freud recommended that psychoanalysts model themselves after a surgeon "who puts aside all his feelings, even his human sympathy, and concentrates his mental forces on the single aim of performing the operation as skillfully as possible" (1912/1958a, p. 115). Furthermore, "The doctor should be opaque to his patients and, like a mirror, should show them nothing but what is shown to him" (p. 118). The various rules that Freud outlined in his papers on technique eventually evolved into three rules for classical analytic technique: neutrality, anonymity, and abstinence (Gabbard, 2005).

Neutrality means that the psychoanalyst should not side with a particular part of the patient's experience (Gabbard, 2005). If a patient, for instance, is unsure about whether or not to leave his job, the neutral psychoanalyst should listen intently, without offering an opinion about the matter. Anonymity refers to the rule that the psychoanalyst should not disclose personal information about him or herself to the patient (Gabbard, 2005). Last, abstinence means that the psychoanalyst should refrain from gratifying the patient's wishes and simply listen to and interpret the meaning of the free associations (Gabbard, 2005). For instance, if a patient asks whether the psychoanalyst thought that she was smart, the psychoanalyst should not gratify the request by offering an opinion. Although there is evidence that Freud regularly violated all of these rules (Gay, 1988), American psychoanalysts took these mandates very seriously. This is the reason that mid-century American psychoanalysts often behaved in ways that seemed stoic, removed, and unfeeling (Gill, 1994).

Freud's technical recommendations for knowing patients seem very odd, indeed. Essentially, he recommended that psychoanalysts should refuse to disclose personal information, withhold judgment on anything that patients say, and refrain from granting requests. All of these technical recommendations are enacted while the psychoanalysts sits, rarely speaking, behind the couch and out of the patient's view. How can this possibly be a good way to get to know someone?

Consider how different Freud's recommendations are from our usual, intuitive way of getting to know others. If I want to know someone, I will usually ask them questions, offer my opinion about what they have said, and readily disclose personal information. The other person usually acts the same way, and we leave the interaction feeling as if we know each other better. Why do Freud's recommendations about coming to know someone differ so radically from the way that we come to know people in ordinary life?

Two features of Freud's mindset must be understood to answer this question. The first is Freud's implicit response to the question "What does it mean to know a client?" For Freud, to know a client meant to know the content of the client's unconscious. Second, Freud operated in an era of high modernism, and considered himself a scientist (Gay, 1988). Modernist ideological assumptions about knowing strongly influenced his technical recommendations. Modernism and the psychoanalytic goal of knowing the unconscious must be understood to appreciate Freud's technical recommendations.

The basic assumption of modernism is that human beings can come to know objective truths about reality (Hansen, 2004). The method for ascertaining these objective truths is science (Anderson, 1990). One of the cornerstones of scientific investigation is that observers must not contaminate, influence, or interfere with, the scientific process. Otherwise, the findings will not be objective (Hansen, 2006b). Scientists employ various methodological strategies to ensure that their subjective biases do not intrude upon their scientific data. For instance, when testing the effectiveness of a new medicine, a double-blind methodology (Ary, Jacobs & Sorensen, 2010) is often employed. One group, for example, may be instructed to take a pill that contains a new medicine, while another group may be instructed to take a placebo pill. Conditions are put into place to ensure that neither the subjects nor the person distributing the pills know which subjects are receiving the medicine and which ones are receiving the placebo. By instituting these "blind" conditions, the risk that the results will be influenced by the biases of the subjects or the person who distributes the pills is severely reduced.

During Freud's lifetime, astonishing discoveries, in medicine, physics, chemistry, and many other fields, which had a direct impact on human betterment, were made with the use of the scientific method. Due to these discoveries, the scientific method became idealized at the turn of the century as a way to uncover the secrets of the universe. Freud, being a product of these times, strongly identified with the role of a scientist (Gay, 1988).

Freud applied this scientific mindset to his goal of unlocking the mysteries of the unconscious. Freud's technical recommendations for coming to know clients were designed to ensure scientific objectivity, analogous to a double-blind methodology. Specifically, Freud recommended that psychoanalysts take a neutral stance so that the free flowing speech of the patient would not be influenced by the biases of the psychoanalyst (Gabbard, 2005).

Anonymity, as a technical recommendation, was put into place so that the patient would be able to project pure transference on the anonymous psychoanalyst (Gabbard, 2005). If psychoanalysts were to disclose personal information, Freud thought that the patient's perception of the psychoanalyst would be influenced by these disclosures instead of being a pure product of transference. For instance, suppose a psychoanalyst disclosed something seemingly benign, such as the type of car that she drives. The patient, who perceives this car as a vehicle that only rich people drive, subsequently says that the therapist could not possibly relate to a lower-middle class person like himself. Subsequently, the patient's perception that the psychoanalyst will never be able to understand him becomes a central issue in the therapy. It would be impossible to discern the degree to which this perception emanated from early developmental issues (i.e., transference) versus simply being a response to the psychoanalyst's disclosure. Even if the psychoanalyst were certain that this perception was fundamentally a transference issue, it would probably be difficult to convince the patient of this fact because the patient could always cite the psychoanalyst's disclosure as the reason for his concern.

The principal of abstinence was also put into place to protect the scientific purity of the psychoanalytic process (Gabbard, 2005). Specifically, the early psychoanalysts theorized that gratifying the transference would inevitably interfere with the process of analyzing it (Gabbard, 2010). For example, suppose a patient asks her psychoanalyst whether the psychoanalyst thinks that she is smart. If the psychoanalyst gratifies the request by answering in the affirmative, the patient, reassured by the response, may never bring up the issue again. However, if the psychoanalyst refuses to answer, the uncertainty and frustration that the patient will experience from the lack of a response will cause this issue to emerge in full force, thereby making its developmental origins analyzable. Gratification, then, was thought by traditional psychoanalysts to cover up transference, while abstinence would cause it to emerge (Gabbard, 2010).

For Freud, then, knowing a client meant to know the client's unconscious. Freud's seemingly bizarre recommendations make sense in the context of his goal of illuminating the unconscious and his thoroughly modernist ideology. Many (probably most) contemporary psychoanalysts reject Freud's original technical guidelines (e.g., Gill, 1994) for reasons that are discussed in upcoming chapters. However, traditional psychoanalytic ideas have had a lasting impact, even influencing humanism, an orientation that made its mark by rejecting foundational psychoanalytic assumptions.

Rogers and Humanism

Like psychoanalysis, psychological humanism is a fascinating theory of subjectivity that gave rise to specific recommendations for helping people who are emotionally troubled. While the Freudian mark on humanism is not hard to detect, founding humanists, ironically, repudiated the very foundation of psychoanalysis (and behaviorism). This is what led some to refer to humanism as the "third force" (DeCarvalho, 1990, p. 22) in psychology, with psychoanalysis and behaviorism being the first two forces. Like psychoanalysis, the humanistic answer to "What does it mean to know a client?" cannot be adequately understood unless one has a sense of the historical and philosophical forces that gave rise to psychological humanism.

The psychological humanism that emerged during the mid-twentieth century is a manifestation of an ideology that dates back many centuries. Renaissance humanists, for instance, rejected the notions that human beings should be understood from a divine perspective (i.e., as God's creations) or as scientific objects (Tarnas, 1991). There is something unique and essential about human experiences, the Renaissance humanists argued, that is lost when it is reduced to other phenomena. For instance, feelings of love can be reduced to biochemical processes or be understood as a manifestation of God's love. Both of these reductionistic conceptualizations, though, would miss the point. To be adequately understood, love (and other uniquely human experiences) should be considered holistically and not be reduced to baser phenomena.

This humanistic principle of irreducibility was also present in the ideological assumptions of the mid-twentieth century psychological humanists (Davidson, 2000). The psychological humanists rejected psychoanalysis and behaviorism (the two dominant mental health orientations at the time) because these orientations reduced people to psychic structures (i.e., psychoanalysis) and stimulus response contingencies (i.e., behaviorism) (DeCarvalho, 1990). In this regard, Matson (1971), in prototypical humanistic fashion, proclaimed moral outrage at the very idea of reductionism when he wrote that "I know of no greater disrespect of the human subject than to treat him as an object—unless it is to demean that object further by fragmenting it into drives, traits, reflexes, and other mechanical hardware" (p. 7).

In addition to the central idea of irreducibility, humanistic ideology also drew from particular philosophical schools of thought, most notably existentialism and phenomenology (DeCarvalho, 1990; Moss, 2001). Although complex and varied, the central tenants of existentialist thought can be summarized as four self-evident (at least to the existentialists) truths about the human condition: freedom, meaninglessness, death, and isolation (Yalom, 1980). Freedom refers to the fact that human beings have free will; they can make free choices. This freedom, however, is a cruel joke because of the second condition: meaninglessness. Because life does not have any intrinsic meaning, there is nothing to guide human choice. In this regard, the existentialist writer Camus noted that "there is but one truly serious philosophical problem, and that is suicide" (Camus, 1955, p. 3) If life has no inherent meaning, then there is no basis for making one choice over another, including the choice to kill oneself.

If the first two concepts do not put you in a good mood, then the second two will probably not either. The existentialists considered the inevitability of death an inescapable truth with which human beings must contend (Yalom, 1980). Last, people are born alone and die alone. No one can truly know the inner experiences of others, so human beings live in a state of perpetual isolation (when I first read the existentialist's description of the isolated nature of human existence, I was relieved that someone had finally validated a part of my experience that I had sensed my entire life).

On the surface, this dark, European philosophical school of thought would not seem to have anything to do with bright, sunny American humanism. However, only certain elements of existentialism were cut and pasted onto the body of humanistic thought (Hansen, 2000). In keeping with the American character, European ideologies are often reinterpreted in cheery, optimistic ways once they cross the ocean and make their way to United States. The same is true with existentialism.

Existentialist freedom and meaninglessness became Americanized by the humanists as the potential for people to freely create meanings (DeCarvalho, 1990; Halling & Nill, 1995; Hansen, 2000). So, while the existentialists found freedom and meaninglessness a tragic part of the human condition, the American humanists took the same two concepts and spun them into an optimistic narrative: People have the freedom to create meanings in life that are personally fulfilling.

American humanism essentially left the existentialist emphasis on death and isolation out of their ideological mix (DeCarvalho, 1990; Halling & Nill, 1995; Hansen, 2000). Phenomenology, a philosophical system that emphasized subjective experience, was also incorporated into humanism in the form of an idealization of subjectivity and personal meaning systems (Halling & Nill, 1995; Sass, 1989). Last, post-World War II American optimism provided humanism with a hopeful emphasis on human potential, growth, and actualization (Halling & Nill, 1995).

With all of these pieces in place, humanism began to have a major influence on mental health culture during the mid-twentieth century (Elkins, 2009). There was a strong contrast between humanism and the dominant orientations of the time (i.e., psychoanalysis and behaviorism). Humanism emphasized irreducibility, free will, and human potential, while psychoanalysis and behaviorism reduced human beings to baser processes, were thoroughly deterministic, and focused on psychopathology (Hansen, 2005a).

Humanistic practitioners derived treatment guidelines from their ideology. Like psychoanalysis, the most fertile ground for understanding the humanistic response to the question "What does it mean to know a client?" lies in the humanistic recommendations for treatment. The person who unquestionably contributed the most to formulating humanistic treatment methods was Carl Rogers.

In his classic, and highly influential, article, "The Necessary and Sufficient Conditions of Therapeutic Personality Change," Rogers (1957) outlined the core conditions of the humanistic treatment scenario. As indicated by the title of his paper, Rogers presumed that these conditions were all that were needed to promote client change. In terms of the specific conditions that counselors must establish to make treatment effective, Rogers advocated that the counselor should be "a congruent, genuine, integrated person" (p. 97) who is "freely and deeply himself" (p. 97). The counselor must also show "a warm acceptance of each aspect of the client's experience" (p. 98), a condition Rogers referred to as "unconditional positive regard" (p. 98). Last, and probably most relevant to the question of knowing, is that counselors must have "an accurate, empathic understanding" (p. 99) of their clients. Rogers presumed that if counselors established these treatment conditions, clients would resume their natural course toward growth, fulfillment, and actualization that had been developmentally interrupted.

These conditions for human relating seem much more intuitively plausible than the Freudian conditions. In this regard, if I meet someone new and would like to get to know them, I will try to present myself in a genuine way, attempt to accept and learn about what the other person is telling me, and show some signs that I have understood their experience. Rogers, therefore, presented a model that is much closer to the natural way that people come to know each other than the psychoanalytic recommendations for knowing. Notably, some critics (e.g., Masson, 1994) have argued that the Rogerian conditions are artificial, false, and intrinsically nongenuine. No one, Masson (1994) argued, can genuinely adopt an attitude of unconditional positive regard toward every client, a fact that, for Masson, makes the Rogerian conditions nothing more than "playacting" (p. 232).

Playacting or not, the Rogerian treatment conditions betray the humanistic mindset about what it means to know a client. For instance, in contrast to Freudian knowing, which presumes the existence of entire realms of human experience that are difficult or impossible to access (i.e., unconscious), humanistic knowing has no inherent limitations; the complete individual can potentially be known through empathy. This presumption of the possibility of full knowing is a byproduct of the humanistic ideal of irreducibility.

The Freudians reduced the psyche, chopping it up into topographic realms, psychic structures, and self and object representations. This reductionist map of the mind provided the Freudians with a basis for claiming that certain psychic realms were less accessible than others. The humanists, in contrast, abhorred reductionism. Therefore, there was no basis for the humanists to claim that various parts of the mind had differential levels of accessibility because, for humanists, there were no parts. This humanistic assumption of irreducibility made full knowing a theoretical possibility.

This emphasis on full knowing, though, is not without its problems. For instance, Sass (1989) noted that the humanistic assumption of psychological transparency conflicts with the private nature of subjectivity. Specifically, is it conceivable that we could all have internal, private, psychological universes, yet those universes could also be completely transparent and knowable to an interested, empathic observer? This, indeed, seems like a contradiction in humanistic ideology. Any theory that idealizes subjectivity would also seem to require related theoretical assumptions about the private nature of internal experience, along with limits on the degree to which that experience could be known (Hansen, 2006c).

This humanistic emphasis on irreducibility and psychological transparency also means that people are capable of knowing and reporting the full contents of their psyche (Sass, 1989). For example, if a client says, "I hate my boss," a humanistic therapist would assume that this is an honest report of the person's experience of the boss. In contrast, a psychoanalytic therapist would wonder whether the statement was a disguised, defended version of some unconscious conflict, such as the client's feelings about his father which were displaced onto the boss. Psychoanalysts, then, have been said to operate under a "hermeneutics of suspicion" (King, 1986, p. 29), because whatever the client says is presumed to be representative of something deeper in the psyche that is not consciously accessible.

In this regard, when I first became a professor in a humanistically-oriented counseling program, I found it very odd that my fellow professors often had their students write self-reflective papers and engage in other introspective tasks as part of the course requirements. During my psychoanalytic training, no self-reflective tasks were ever mandated as part of a course. Eventually, I came to understand that these different approaches to education were most likely derived from the theoretical cultures of the training programs (Hansen, 2009b). In my psychoanalytically-oriented graduate school, self-reflection in the classroom would have been seen as useless because (in keeping with psychoanalytic assumptions) all independent, introspective conclusions are inevitably defensive, self-deceptions. The only way to get past these self-deceptions is to become the client of a psychoanalytically-oriented psychotherapist, who could point out the various ways that you were avoiding the real issues. For humanists, of course, self-deception is not an intrinsic part of human experience. Therefore, in humanistically oriented training programs, personal growth can occur from conscious self-reflection.

Notably, humanistic and psychoanalytic ideologies share a fundamentally modernist base (Hansen, 2006a). That is, proponents of both schools of thought presumed that therapists could come to know objective truths about clients. Traditional psychoanalysts believed that they could accurately infer the unconscious contents of their patients' psyches. Humanists, on the other hand, emphasized the importance of "*accurate*, empathic understanding" (Rogers, 1957, p. 99; Italics added). For both schools of thought, then, therapists are capable of accurately knowing clients if the correct methods are employed.

In keeping with the modernist, scientific template, both humanists and psychoanalysts had methods for keeping the influence of the counselor from contaminating the psychological productions of the client. Traditional psychoanalysts essentially mimicked the detached, objective posture of a scientist so that the data (i.e., patient verbalizations) would not be influenced by the observer (i.e., psychoanalyst). Humanists, in contrast, placed an emphasis on understanding whatever the client presented (Rogers, 1986). By simply trying to understand what the client presents, without adding the counselor's agenda into the process, the humanists presumed that the contaminating influence of the therapist would be kept to a minimum. For traditional psychoanalysts and humanists, then, clients were analogous to data producing experiments and therapists were scientific observers.

Therefore, although humanism and psychoanalysis have very different answers to the question "What does it mean to know a client?" both theoretical orientations were founded on a scientific ideological template. Notably, certain contemporary schools of psychoanalytic thought (e.g., intersubjective movement) have rejected the traditional modernist conceptualization of the therapeutic scenario. In subsequent chapters, the consequences of rejecting the modernist foundation of traditional orientations to psychotherapy are explored.

Theoretical Integration of Psychoanalysis and Humanism

Despite their modernist commonality, there are some seemingly insurmountable theoretical differences between psychoanalysis and humanism. These differences result in very different views about what it means to know a client. As I mentioned in the description of my background, my graduate training was strictly psychoanalytic. However, when I began working as a professor shortly after graduating, I was suddenly thrust into a Rogerian, humanistic milieu where psychoanalytic ideas were generally not taken seriously. Although humanistic concepts were somewhat foreign to me at the time, I felt a strong kinship with the humanistic mission of attempting to know the subjective life of clients. The common goal of both psychoanalysis and humanism is thorough knowledge of subjectivity, placing individual meaning systems above all other considerations. However, these theories have very different assumptions about human minds and how to access them, which, again, results in divergent, and arguably incompatible, conclusions about what it means to know a client.

Ideally, I reasoned, some sort of integration between psychoanalysis and humanism could be formulated to harness the power of both orientations to know and help clients. This integration could potentially occur on at least two levels. At a technical level, for instance, practitioners, in eclectic fashion, could use techniques and practice recommendations from both theoretical camps without regard for grand theoretical unification. This technical integration, although worthy in its own right, did not have the potential to satisfy my need to integrate humanism and psychoanalysis at a theoretical level. I reasoned that an internally consistent, theoretical integration might result in a super theory of knowing and helping because it would capitalize on the insights of both orientations.

The problem with integrating humanism and psychoanalysis into a super theory, though, is that these orientations have radically different foundational assumptions about human nature. Traditional psychoanalysis proceeds from the assumption that people begin life as seething cauldrons of sexual and aggressive drives. When these drives come into conflict with internalized societal mandates, as they inevitably do, wishes and fantasies connected with the drives are repressed. Compromises must be struck between unconscious mental life and the demands of civilization (Freud, 1930/1961a), a process that can result in symptoms (Arlow & Brenner, 1964). Humanism, alternatively, posits that people have an inborn capacity for positive growth and self-actualization, which can be derailed by certain developmental occurrences (Hansen, 2000). By establishing the "necessary and sufficient" (Rogers, 1957, p. 95) relational conditions, counselors can help clients get back on the track to self-actualization. Therefore, although humanism and psychoanalysis both idealize subjective meaning systems, these orientations have radically different starting assumptions, which make them seemingly incompatible at the level of their theoretical DNA.

Despite these challenges, when I was initially exposed to humanism I thought that the only intellectually satisfying way to harness the power of psychoanalysis and humanism would be to formulate some sort of grand theoretical unification. After all, I reasoned, both orientations help clients, so each of these theories must be partially correct about human nature and subjectivity. If psychoanalysis and humanism could be seamlessly integrated at a theoretical level, this grand, super theory would be far more capable of answering my questions about what it means to know clients and how to help them than either theory could be on its own. I no longer endorse this reasoning, and eventually used other conceptual strategies, which are reviewed later in this book, for capitalizing on the insights of humanism, psychoanalysis, and other helping orientations. However, at the time, I thought that theoretical integration was my only choice.

I started my search for a grand theory of subjectivity by reviewing various attempts to integrate psychoanalysis and humanism at a theoretical level (e.g., Gladding & Yonce, 1986; Kahn, 1985; Sugarman, 1977a, 1977b; Tobin, 1990). Although these attempts provided some interesting food for thought, none of them satisfied my need to develop a seamless, unified theory. I decided to make my own attempt at a theoretical integration of humanism and psychoanalysis, which was eventually published (Hansen, 2000). While I now disagree with some of the initial philosophical assumptions that served as the foundation for this work, I believe that my efforts at integration had interesting implications for the question of what it means to know a client. Therefore, I review these efforts below.

The first step to integrate psychoanalysis and humanism is to recognize that psychoanalysis, itself, is not a unified theory (Pine, 1990). Freud was a prolific writer who regularly revised his theories. Furthermore, subsequent theorists extended and elaborated Freud's ideas and added new conceptual components to the growing body of psychoanalytic thought. As a result, various schools of psychoanalysis, with devoted adherents, were established. Representatives from one school of psychoanalysis often completely dismissed the perspectives of theorists from other schools, which resulted in rigid, dogmatic training programs at psychoanalytic institutes in the mid-twentieth century (Kirsner, 2000). For purposes of theoretical integration, then, psychoanalysis cannot be considered a unified theory.

There are various ways to map psychoanalytic theory into subschools. In my estimation, Pine (1990) has offered a useful and defensible conceptual map by dividing psychoanalytic theory into drive, ego, object, and self domains. Although there are various points of emphasis in humanistic thought, humanism did not become conceptually divided into various competing schools with different foundational assumptions like psychoanalysis. Therefore, a reasonable strategy to accomplish the goal of theoretical unification is to systematically compare each of the psychoanalytic schools of thought with humanism in the hopes of capitalizing on some conceptual commonalities.

The first psychoanalytic school to emerge was drive theory (Pine, 1990). Freud (1900/1953) posited a topographic model of the mind, which was divided into unconscious, pre-conscious, and conscious realms. While people are aware of their conscious mental life and can turn their attention to the pre-conscious, the unconscious realm contains actively repressed, libidinally charged psychosexual wishes from childhood that are inaccessible to introspection. These wishes, because they are charged with psychic energy, can reemerge in derivative form to cause psychological symptoms. By decoding the psychically determined hidden messages in free associations and transference manifestations, psychoanalysts presumed that they could infer the contents of the unconscious mental life of their clients. These are the primary assumptions of drive theory, which emerged at the beginning of the twentieth century.

Out of all of the four schools of psychoanalysis identified by Pine (1990), humanism is the least compatible with drive theory. This incompatibility is because the basic tenets of drive theory require that virtually any client manifestation be reduced to latent drives and the psychosexual conflicts associated with them (Hansen, 2000). For instance, in one of his case studies, Freud posited that the Oedipal conflict and castration anxiety were at the root of a young boy's fear of horses (Freud, 1909/1955). This type of wholesale reduction of human experience to primary, universal conflicts associated with the drives is virtually the opposite of the humanistic idealization of unreduced conscious experience. However, free association, the psychoanalytic method used to gain access to subjective life, was designed to give full expressive reign to clients. This emphasis on unbridled self-expression has some correspondence with humanistic ideals, which also emphasize the thorough communication of subjective states to the psychotherapist (Hansen, 2000). However, particularly during the period when drive theory was intro-duced, most psychoanalysts were probably not listening to the free associa-tions to learn about the nuances of subjective life. Rather, they were likely retrofitting the content of free associations into Freud's psychosexual theo-ries, a reductionist style of listening that is incompatible with the holistic ideal of humanism.

Ego psychology, a variant of psychoanalytic theory that emerged in the 1920s, drew from Freud's (1923/1961b) structural model of the mind, which divided the psyche into id, ego, and superego. Freud's observations that defense mechanisms were unconscious and that his patients often had a guilty, self-punitive component to their psyches, led him to formulate the psychic structures that characterize the structural model (Arlow & Brenner, 1964). Placing the id, ego, and superego onto a map of the mind created two important new emphases in psychoanalytic ideology and treatment: (a) de-fense (i.e., the mechanisms a person uses to protect him or herself from experiencing the anxiety that results from the emergence of repressed id contents; and (b) adaptation (i.e., the degree to which the defensive compro-mises result in a happy, fulfilled life) (Arlow & Brenner, 1964).

Like drive theory, ego psychology was mechanistic and reductionistic. However, ego psychology included greater theoretical tools than drive theory for understanding the ways in which people protect themselves from experi-encing psychological distress. With this emphasis on defensive maneuvers, ego psychology arguably widened the phenomenological scope of psycho-analysis to include an important element of subjectivity. Therefore, while the reductionism of ego psychology clearly has a strong element of incompatibil-ity with the holistic emphasis of humanism, the new attentiveness to the nuances of self-protection that came with ego psychology arguably brought psychoanalysis closer to the humanistic ideal of appreciating and understand-ing the totality of subjective life (Hansen, 2000).

As opposed to the drives and structures of the previous theories of psychoanalysis, object relations theory highlighted the importance of attach-ment and internalized self-other relationships (Pine, 1990). Throughout de-velopment, conflictual relational paradigms are internalized and repressed. These paradigms can become activated in later life, thereby causing psycho-logical distress. For example, suppose that during development a girl inter-nalizes an image of her father as rejecting and abandoning her. As a compo-nent of this unconscious relational paradigm, she may attribute her father's attitude to personal failings or her unworthiness as a daughter. As an adult, this object relations paradigm may be unconsciously enacted with men, thereby causing the woman to experience difficulties in romantic relation-ships. Like drive and ego psychology, various theoretical perspectives emerged within the object relations movement. However, the determinative role of internalized self-other relational paradigms is the foundation of object relations psychology.

The emphasis on relationships and attachment make object relations theory far more compatible with humanism than either drive or ego psychology. The reduction of client experience to object relations paradigms is, of course, at least somewhat incompatible with the humanistic idealization of unreduced conscious experience. However, because it trades the mechanistic elements of drive and ego psychology for the experiential richness of relationships, object relations theory undoubtedly has greater conceptual congruence with humanistic ideology than the first two psychologies of psychoanalysis (Hansen, 2000).

Self psychology, a psychoanalytic movement that emerged in the early 1970s, emphasizes the ongoing development of a sense of self (Pine, 1990). Kohut (1971) posited an elaborate theory of self-development and detailed the narcissistic psychopathology that can result when this development goes awry. Self psychology gradually evolved into an independent school of psychoanalytic thought, which highlighted the importance of self-experiences, empathy as a method of knowing, and the ways in which deficiencies in self structure can result in psychopathology (Pine, 1990). Like the other theories of psychoanalysis, there are many theoretical details and controversies within the self psychology movement. However, an emphasis on the self structure as an overarching explanatory principle is the common feature of all self psychological theorizing.

Self psychology arguably has a greater degree of theoretical compatibility with humanism than drive, ego, or object relations psychology. By collapsing human experience into the self structure, self psychology, like the other three psychoanalytic schools of thought, has a reductionistic element. However, this reductionism is somewhat offset by the self psychological emphasis on self experience and knowing through empathy. These theoretical features make self psychology a closer conceptual kin to humanism than the other theories of psychoanalysis (Hansen, 2000).

Although psychoanalytic schools of thought have some points of correspondence with humanism, seamless theoretical integration of humanism and psychoanalysis would seem to be a conceptual impossibility. Humanism emphasizes the irreducibility of human experience (Davidson, 2000; Matson, 1971), while each of the four psychoanalytic orientations have a reductionistic element (Hansen, 2000). Perhaps, however, there is a way to fashion an integration of these orientations that does not require a forceful pounding of the round peg of psychoanalysis into the square hole of humanism. In this regard, consider that psychoanalysis, as it evolved from drive through self psychology, increasingly emphasized the primacy of subjective experience. Turn-of-the-century drive theory is highly mechanistic and reductive. By the

1970s, with the introduction of self psychology, psychoanalytic thought highlighted the importance of subjective experiences and empathy as a means of knowing (Hansen, 2000). Humanism, in reverse fashion, began with the idealization of authentic encounters, but evolved to include certain structural, reductive elements, such as diagnostics (e.g., Bohart, 1990) and micro-skills training (Truax & Carkhuff, 1967).

A meta-analysis of the historical development of psychoanalysis and humanism, then, suggests that psychoanalysis became more humanistic, and humanism gradually evolved to incorporate structural elements (Hansen, 2000). These theoretical transitions make sense. No psychological theory of helping can remain exclusively structural and reductionistic because unreduced experiential factors eventually have to be taken into account in order to understand and help people. Likewise, treatment orientations cannot simply advocate authentic encounters and genuine relating, because this directive does not provide sufficient guidance or structure for coming to know someone.

With this in mind, an integration of humanism and psychoanalysis can occur on a continuum of knowing (Hansen, 2000). One end of the continuum is highly structured, with universal laws of the mind and other trappings of reductionism. The other end of the continuum is characterized by an emphasis on authentic encounters with unreduced subjective experiences. Over time, theories that start at one end of the continuum begin to transition to the other, as neither of the endpoints, on their own, provide sufficient guidance for knowing.

Furthermore, this continuum of knowing is arguably reflected in the experiential side of the work of counselors and psychotherapists (Hansen, 2000). Helping professionals come to know their clients by alternating between a mindset that is receptive to the raw products of inner life and a mode of experiencing that structures client communications according to reductive, psychological principles. Alternations between careful listening and conceptualizing is a regular part of coming to know clients. The historical development of psychoanalysis and humanism, then, mirrors the knowing processes that are an inherent component of the helping process (Hansen, 2000). This continuum of knowing can be used to provide a partial answer to the central question of this chapter. Perhaps knowing a client, or anyone for that matter, necessarily means understanding her or him according to some combination of authentic relating and reductive conceptual categories.

DISCUSSION AND CONCLUSIONS

Although there are numerous helping orientations, psychoanalysis and humanism, as comprehensive theories of subjectivity, arguably have the most complete and compelling answers to the question, "What does it mean to know a client?" Knowing is the foundational starting point of psychoanalytic and humanistic theory. Both theories hold out the enticing, hopeful promise of human knowing, albeit with very different assumptions about what knowing entails.

The vital role of knowing clients in psychoanalytic thought led Freud and his followers to develop numerous maps of the mind. The implicit assumption behind these theoretical efforts is that mapping the psychic terrain makes knowing a possibility, just as a geographical map can be considered vital to the process of coming to know a particular area. Wandering around aimlessly, either in the psyche or on land, might not allow full knowing to occur. After all, traditional psychoanalysts might argue, how could one find or recognize anything without a map?

Traditional humanists, alternatively, drew from an entirely different value system about knowing. For humanists, a map was an impediment to knowing, not a means to facilitate it. It is easy to appreciate this reasoning. To apply a geographical analogy to this humanistic value system, perhaps the best way to come to know a city, for instance, is to wander through it with no particular plan, randomly encounter people and places, and refuse to allow some rigid guide to control the experience. This humanistic way of knowing could arguably provide much more intimate information than the structured maps of psychoanalysis.

Troubling challenges, though, can be raised against both the humanistic and psychoanalytic value systems about knowing. A challenge to the humanists, for instance, might be that it is naive to presume that people can operate without a map. People have experiential templates that organize and give meaning to incoming experiences. If it were not for these templates, every experience would be completely new. One would have to relearn that it is dangerous to step out in front of traffic, for example, upon encountering every new busy road. Given that these templates and accompanying perceptual biases are an intrinsic part of being human, client communications are always reductively categorized according to the psychological templates of the psychotherapist. Arguably, it would be better to be honest about this reductionism than to engage in theoretical denial.

One of the obvious challenges that can be raised about psychoanalytic knowing is whether the maps of the mind generated by psychoanalytic theorists are accurate. Many of the psychoanalytic maps conflict with one another (e.g., ego psychology and self psychology), which makes skepticism about accuracy a reasonable concern. Indeed, how could the accuracy of a psychic map ever be verified? With a geographical map, accuracy can be assessed by the degree of correspondence to the tangible terrain. However, given the intangible nature of the psyche, what evidence could possibly serve to verify that psychoanalytic maps are accurate? They cannot be checked against any tangible terrain. For the sake of argument, suppose that this obvious problem were ignored, and it was somehow known that certain psychoanalytic maps of the mind were accurate. Even given this completely implausible hypothetical assumption, following an accurate guide to the psyche would certainly cause one to miss certain elements of the mind, just as following an accurate map of geographical territory inevitably causes one to overlook sights that are not highlighted by the map. What if the psychic sights missed by this hypothetical, accurate psychoanalytic map happen to be the important ones?

Despite these theoretical problems and contradictions, both psychoanalysis and humanism, in their own ways, place the highest value on knowing clients. Thus, these orientations are uniquely qualified to address the question "what does it mean to know a client?" Alternative theoretical systems do not begin with the assumption that full knowing is desirable or possible. Therefore, they do not provide sufficient epistemological substance to fuel an inquiry process about knowing.

For example, existentialism has many of the same theoretical features as humanism. Formal existentialism, however, includes the assumption that isolation is an intrinsic part of human nature; no one can ever be fully known or gain complete knowledge about others (Yalom, 1980). This epistemological pessimism, though it may seem intuitively correct, does not provide the proper foundation for an extended discussion about what it means to know clients. Other theories idealize certain phenomenon as highly important to know and completely dismiss others. Cognitive-behaviorists, for instance, idealize knowledge about thought processes but severely minimize the importance of other experiential factors (Mahoney, 1991). Traditional behaviorists outright reject the entire black box of the mind and focus their efforts on knowing stimulus-response contingencies (Skinner, 1974). The webs of personal meaning within which the idealized phenomenon occur are dismissed as clinically insignificant by theoretical systems that narrowly define the range of what it is important to know. Again, as orientations that advocate a thorough knowing of subjectivity, psychoanalysis and humanism are uniquely qualified to address the question of what it means to know clients.

Notably, however, the presumption that people are locked into cranial prisons is only one, perhaps arbitrary, way to conceptualize the human condition. This individualistic assumption is the conceptual starting point for all traditional theories of helping. Social constructionism, as an example of an alternative system of thought, rejects the presumption of isolated individualism and emphasizes the communal construction of meaning (Gergen, 1999). Therefore, the question about what it means to know clients may merely be fruit from a particular philosophical tree. If it were not for the strong value placed on individualism in Western culture, questions about knowing others might seem trivial or bizarre.

This Western emphasis on individualism can be traced back to at least the Enlightenment. In the late seventeenth century, Enlightenment philosophers, such as Locke, Descartes, and Bacon, emphasized reason as the primary means of answering fundamental questions about the human condition (Hicks, 2004). Descartes (1988), for instance, started his philosophical system with radical doubt, questioning everything he had learned, even the assumption that he existed. Through a series of introspective, carefully reasoned meditations, Descartes developed a logical proof that verified his own existence. This verification served as the starting point for a philosophical system that divided the world into immaterial (i.e., the mind) and material ontological domains (Custance & Travis, 1980; Stolorow, Atwood, & Orange, 2002).

The Enlightenment emphasis on reason, along with the introspective method for drawing conclusions, resulted in a strong Western tradition of individualism. Reason is a property of individuals, so individualism is a natural consequence of philosophical systems that idealize reason as a method of knowing (Hicks, 2004). Under the influence of these philosophical assumptions, the Western self gradually became more prominent and interiorized (Anderson, 1990; Flax, 1990; Messer & Warren, 2001). The captain of every individual ship became locked away in the hull of the skull, forever inaccessible to outsiders.

Without this emphasis on individualism, which, again, is perhaps a by-product of an arbitrary set of philosophical assumptions, the question of what it means to know a client might seem nonsensical. Certainly the question could not even be formulated outside of a set of starting assumptions that idealize individualism. To illustrate this point, imagine that, in an alternate universe, people have been indoctrinated into a set of philosophical assumptions, which seem perfectly reasonable to them, that naturally lead them to ask "what is the color of laughter?" This question seems as obvious and important to philosophically minded representatives from this alternative universe as the question about knowing others seems to Western intellectuals.

It is perhaps disturbing to think that the Western intellectual tradition, and, by extension, all traditional systems of psychotherapy, might have been built up from a completely arbitrary foundation. Indeed, are there any foundations that are truly foundational, in the sense of being universally true? Or, have human beings simply constructed interesting, but always arbitrary, ideas throughout the course of history? Is it possible to answer these questions about foundations? Indeed, is it even worthwhile to pursue these issues? Perhaps it would be better to ignore them altogether. These questions, which some consider inherently unanswerable, dry, and lifeless, usually belong to the discipline of philosophy. In subsequent chapters, I invite these, and other, philosophical questions into the counseling relationship, wherein they come to life, blossom, and create exciting, new possibilities for the "suffering strangers" (Orange, 2011, p. 37) who come to us for help.

Chapter Four

What Makes Counseling Effective?

Two people sit in a room. One, who came seeking relief from psychological suffering, does most of the talking. As the designated helper, the other listens intently and occasionally makes a remark. Over a period of months, the two meet for a total of twelve hours. The only activity that takes place during these meetings is a series of conversations between the two participants. After the twelfth meeting, the sufferer reports that she is suffering far less than when she first came to meet with the helper.

The above scenario has occurred regularly for over a century. There is strong empirical evidence that counseling, indeed, helps people (Wampold, 2001). In fact, people who participate in psychotherapy consistently report receiving tremendous benefit (Seligman, 1995). What, though, are the precise ingredients in the counseling scenario that are responsible for the helping effect? This is a very difficult question to answer because there are numerous factors at work during counseling, just as there are in any relational exchange.

For instance, it could be the specialized techniques that counselors employ, such as cognitive reframing or interpretation of unconscious conflict, which are responsible for client change. On the other hand, perhaps the relationship with the counselor is responsible for positive outcomes and techniques have little to do with it. Alternatively, maybe it is something about the personal qualities of the counselor that bring about the helping effect. As another possibility, perhaps clients get better simply because they come to believe that change is possible, which would make the entire counseling scenario an elaborate placebo. I could continue this list and name dozens of other possibilities.

However, the elements that make up human interaction are so rich, interwoven, and inseparable that it would seem virtually impossible to experi-

mentally isolate the factors that are responsible for positive changes in counseling. In contrast, a medical researcher, after learning that a multi-ingredient
compound has a therapeutic effect, might be able to isolate each of the
ingredients and test them independently to determine which one is responsible for the benefit. How, though, can counseling techniques ever be experi-
mentally separated from the relationship in which they are administered? Can
the rich set of interwoven elements that contribute to any human interaction
ever be isolated and tested independently?

To add a further, more philosophical, component to the effectiveness
question, how should effective helping be defined? What, precisely, constitutes a good therapeutic outcome? Traditional psychoanalysts would argue
that the only good therapeutic outcome is structural personality change (e.g.,
Brenner, 1973). Once client personality has been changed by a thorough
working through of defenses and archaic object relations patterns, symptom
remission will likely follow. Indeed, during my training I was taught that
psychoanalytic treatment provides great benefit to clients even if the therapy
does not result in a reduction of symptoms. The benefit is that clients will
have acquired conscious knowledge of conflicts that were formerly unconscious, thereby freeing them to make fully informed, realistic choices about
their lives rather than reflexively responding to unconscious processes.

This reasoning has always struck me as suspiciously self-serving for practitioners who make their living by seeing clients for extended periods of time
and who may not want to be bothered by accountability. Nevertheless, I was
educationally indoctrinated into these psychoanalytic assumptions. On one
occasion during my training, I reported on the status of one of my clients to
my supervisor. After about ten sessions, the client had decided to discontinue
therapy because the problems that had led him to seek treatment had been
successfully resolved. Upon hearing this, my supervisor smiled knowingly
and said "transference cure." My supervisor meant that it was impossible for
structural, personality change to have occurred in such a brief period of time.
Therefore, the supposed cure was merely an illusion because it was completely dependent on external, relational factors in the therapy rather than
being determined by internal, psychological changes in the client. Even
though my client had reported that treatment had been a success, my supervisor, who presumed to know better, had deemed it a failure.

At the other end of the spectrum, traditional behaviorists judge the success of treatment according to a strict, quantitative accounting of the degree
to which problematic behaviors have been reduced. If a client wanted to quit
smoking, was afraid to travel by plane, or was prone to angry outbursts, the
only reasonable definition of treatment success for behaviorists is whether
these measurable problems improve. Like the psychoanalytic perspective on
treatment effectiveness, this behavioral conceptualization seems inadequate
in some respects. Most people do not come to helping professionals with

discrete, behavioral complaints. Psychological problems are usually complex, co-occurring, and multi-faceted. Some problems, such as depression, necessarily involve internal distress and are not ordinarily caused by discrete, behavioral emissions. Furthermore, for most people, a feeling that meaningful change has occurred probably involves a sense that something psychological has shifted, not merely that a bothersome behavior had been eliminated.

Despite these problems with empirically identifying the factors that contribute to effectiveness and defining what effectiveness entails, the question of "what makes counseling effective?" is clearly vitally important for helping professionals to address. This question also has personal significance for me.

PERSONAL AND PROFESSIONAL
SIGNIFICANCE OF THE QUESTION

As I mentioned previously, I deliberately sought out a doctoral program in psychology that had a strong psychoanalytic orientation. Out of all of the theorists to whom I had been exposed, Freud's ideas intrigued me the most (by far). I thought that six years of intensive psychoanalytic study with Freudian professors would satisfy my need to master psychoanalytic ideas and practice. In retrospect, I am glad that I made the choice that I did. However, I did not really know what I was getting myself into at the time.

To say that my graduate program was psychoanalytically oriented would be a gross understatement. Indeed, my clinical professors were strict Freudians who were almost completely intolerant of other modes of thought. The psychology department also employed nonclinical faculty who were exclusively devoted to research, but I simply muddled through their courses just to obtain the degree. They did not have the status, prestige, or influence of the psychoanalytic faculty who ran the program. Within my training program, then, there was only one answer to what makes counseling effective: the psychoanalytic method.

To illustrate the ideological stranglehold that the clinical professors had over the minds of their students, I vividly recall the few times when students innocently proposed that nonpsychoanalytic interventions might be tried with the client whose case was being presented during the case conference class. All of the psychoanalytic gurus who ran that course would inevitably respond in the same way: They would subtly, and sometimes not so subtly, berate the student for proposing the idea. Indeed, I remember when a young professor, who had a cognitive-behavioral orientation, walked into this lion's den. After hearing a case, she made the perfectly reasonable suggestion that some cognitive strategies might be helpful to the client. In response, the senior, psychoanalytic professor treated her very rudely, with active disdain.

I remember feeling sorry for this young professor who apparently did not know enough to decline the invitation to the conference. She never returned.

Later in graduate school, I started to suspect that my psychoanalytic professors might not have cornered the market on the truth about what makes counseling effective. One piece of evidence that I found hard to ignore was the fact that the gurus virtually never agreed with each other. For instance, for the first two years of graduate school, I attended two case conference courses, each of which was taught by a different professor. They both met on the same day of the week, one in the morning and the other in the afternoon. As part of the course requirements, students signed up to present the cases that they were seeing at the university clinic. Not uncommonly, the same case was presented to both the morning and the afternoon professors. Although both gurus were dogmatically psychoanalytic, they virtually always conceptualized the same case differently and recommended completely different treatment interventions.

I remember the dim thought that began to emerge at the periphery of my consciousness: I could not possibly be learning the truth about what makes counseling effective from these professors if they did not agree with each other. Truth is singular, not plural. Which one of them, if any, then, knew the truth? Certainly, they were all very persuasive. I walked away from the morning case conference certain that the perspective of the morning professor was the only reasonable way to interpret the clinical material that had been presented. Then, upon hearing the afternoon professor's cogent justifications for his conceptualizations, I left with a strong sense of certainty that he was correct.

Why, though, given the evidence, did I not question whether my professors knew the truth about what makes counseling effective? Although I was young and intimidated, there had to be other reasons for my reluctance to pose this question. In fact, even in the privacy of my own mind, I could barely tolerate the thought that I might not be learning the truth from them. In this regard, although I sometimes felt sorry for the students and guests who were berated by the gurus, I noticed that I often privately cheered for my abusive professors. How dare someone undermine my education by questioning the wisdom that my professors were trying to impart to me. Not only did I refuse to question what I was being taught, part of me actively identified with the ideological aggressors.

In retrospect, I believe that cognitive dissonance inhibited me from freely thinking and expressing critical thoughts that should have been plainly obvious. Essentially, the theory of cognitive dissonance maintains that it is difficult to hold conflicting thoughts or beliefs at the same time (Festinger, 1957). You can bet that the hundred dollar bottle of wine, for instance, will always taste excellent, even before you pop the cork. This is because it is difficult to reconcile the simultaneous thoughts of paying a lot of money for something and being disappointed by the results. I had invested a tremendous amount of time, money, and energy into graduate school. I had bet my entire future on my education. Under those circumstances, the thought that my professors might not know what they were talking about was virtually impossible to entertain. In fact, for me, the only safe, comfortable option was to idealize the gurus and try to follow them, even if what they said did not make much sense. I later learned that it was common for training programs to dogmatically advocate a specific orientation, especially during the era when I was trained (Fancher, 1995). Psychoanalytic institutes, in particular, were notorious for their theoretical dogmatism (Kirsner, 2000).

I was able to maintain my comfortable, psychoanalytic mindset even after I graduated. At the psychiatric hospital where I worked, I was assigned a psychoanalytically oriented supervisor, who fed me the same party line that I had bought during graduate school. I graduated, but I had not escaped the ideological cocoon. Once I became a professor, though, the pressures to recognize alternative orientations were too great to ignore.

Several years after graduation, I accepted a professorial position in a department of counseling. I found the professional culture of counseling warm, open, and accepting, which was a refreshing change from the militaristic, hierarchical culture of my old psychology program. I loved everything about the job. There was only one problem: My new colleagues did not care for psychoanalysis. In fact, they often openly berated it. To make my dilemma worse, counselors, with their humanistic methods, were obviously very helpful to their clients. In my observation, they were just as helpful, if not more so, than psychoanalytic practitioners.

At the time, it was impossible for me to come up with an explanation for these observations. Psychoanalysis and humanism, although they share certain features, are ideologically opposite in many respects (Hansen, 2000). The theories of change, assumptions about human nature, and methods of intervention of these treatment orientations are completely different and, as far as I could tell, conceptually incompatible. How, then, could they both be effective? If one physician uses antibiotics to treat an infection, and the other uses leeches, the method that is closer to the truth about the cause of and cure for infections will, naturally, be the one with the better outcome. How could two completely opposite perspectives both produce good results?

At the time, I knew other graduates from my old psychology program who had been faced with this same dilemma. Many of them defensively retreated back into psychoanalytic thought and privately accused their colleagues, who endorsed alternative orientations, of only providing "Band-Aid solutions" to their clients' problems. Cognitive-behavioral approaches only covered up problems, they would tell me, while psychoanalysis provided lasting relief by resolving core issues.

There were several factors that prevented me from adopting this resolution. First, it was not consistent with my observations. From what I observed, the clients of humanistic counselors received lasting help, not just Band-Aid solutions. Second, I liked my new colleagues. I did not want to alienate them by grandiosely acting as if I knew the truth about what makes counseling effective, particularly since I did not believe that this was the case. No one wants a grandiose jerk for a colleague. Third, I had achieved enough distance from graduate school so that I no longer felt a strong sense of dissonance about questioning psychoanalytic ideas. After all, even if everything that my professors taught me was false, I secured a job that I loved with my degree. I was so grateful to be happily employed that it no longer mattered to me whether I had been taught the truth about what makes counseling effective. Last, I saw my dissonance as an opportunity. I could finally indulge the oppositional thoughts that I could not bear to entertain during graduate school. Indeed, with my new professorial position, I could actually be paid to explore them! From that point on, I decided to devote a sizable proportion of my scholarly career to obtaining conceptual resolutions to the question "what makes counseling effective?"

I hope that this psychological description of my struggles with psychoanalytic dogmatism is helpful to trainees and professionals who are tied to a particular orientation but sometimes question whether their allegiance is justified. Theoretical orientations are like labyrinths; it can be difficult to find your way out of them. Trainees in the helping professions are often enculturated into a particular theoretical orientation. This enculturation process, along with the inherent ambiguity of the helping scenario, the sacrifices and commitment of resources that advanced training requires, the fact that different orientations to treatment often have completely incompatible assumptions, and the numerous persuasive gurus who do not hesitate to vigorously advocate for their preferred perspectives, make for a difficult, conflictual psychological path for trainees in the helping professions. Unfortunately, the psychological and ideological struggles that trainees endure on the way to becoming mature helping professionals are seldom discussed. The resolution to these struggles, ironically, often results in theoretical dogmatism, which interferes with the ability to objectively consider the question, "what makes counseling effective?"

However, I believe that helping professionals have an obligation to put aside what they have learned, abandon their dogmatic ties, and honestly address the question of what makes counseling effective. When clients come to counseling they are vulnerable and in pain. Under these professional circumstances, counselors must give due consideration to the processes that promote effective change. Out of the four fundamental questions in this book, then, the question considered in this chapter is probably the most important one to consider.

WHAT MAKES COUNSELING EFFECTIVE?

Counseling is a complex endeavor that involves innumerable variables. To add even further complexity to the effectiveness question, the helping process has evolved throughout different cultural contexts and historical periods. Psychotherapeutic endeavors that were considered vitally important to one era of practitioners were sometimes seen as trivial, or even harmful, to therapists during subsequent periods (e.g., recovering repressed memories [Loftus & Ketcham, 1994]). Indeed, counseling has undoubtedly been subject to continual faddism, with orientations coming into favor and then quickly disappearing (e.g., primal scream therapy [Janov, 1970]; transactional analysis [Berne, 1961]). Therapeutic schools of thought, then, did not emerge in a progressive, scientific way. Indeed, the history of psychotherapy is a century long parade of charming, grandiose pioneers who boldly proposed new and creative conceptualizations of psychological problems and what to do about them. Some of these pioneers gained lasting followings, while others quickly faded into obscurity. To adequately answer the question, "what makes counseling effective?" then, the broad historical/cultural context in which psychotherapy emerged must be considered. Some of this material has been covered in the chapter on mental health culture. However, it is worth reviewing in the context of the primary question that is under consideration in this chapter.

The "talking cure" (Gay, 1988, p. 65) was initially developed by Sigmund Freud about a century ago. When Freud first proposed his ideas, such as unconscious motivation and childhood psychosexual conflicts, they were generally dismissed by the intelligentsia as quackery (Gay, 1988). Gradually, however, a group of devoted followers began to endorse psychoanalytic thought. Freud met with a core group of these disciples on a regular basis (Gay, 1988). The atmosphere of these meetings was not characterized by a free exchange of ideas, though. Disagreeing with the master regularly resulted in dismissal from the group. Carl Jung, Freud's heir apparent, and Alfred Adler, were ex-communicated by Freud because they disagreed with certain psychoanalytic assumptions about human nature (Gay, 1988). Both went on to found their own schools of thought. Freud's intolerance of competing ideas set the stage for the ideological dogmatism in psychotherapy culture for decades to come (Fancher, 1995; Kirsner, 2009).

Many of Freud's early followers were Jews. Thus, when the threat of Nazi occupation spread throughout Europe, numerous psychoanalysts fled to the United States to escape persecution (Fancher, 1995; Jacoby, 1983). These immigrant European psychoanalysts took positions at American universities and institutes, which caused psychoanalytic ideas and practice to spread quickly in the United States during the 1940s and 1950s (Jacoby, 1983). Soon after its arrival, though, American psychiatrists took hold of psychoanalytic practice and barred other professions from practicing it (Jacoby, 1983;

Kirsner, 2009; McWilliams, 2004). Freud never intended for a single profession to have exclusive rights to psychoanalytic practice (Freud, 1926/1959). In America, though, the psychiatric guild successfully defined psychoanalysis as a medical practice, which meant that nonpsychiatrists were not legally able to practice it (McWilliams, 2004).

Psychoanalysis also greatly expanded the potential pool of psychiatric patients (Fancher, 1995). Prior to the introduction of psychoanalysis to American culture, psychiatrists generally worked in asylums treating residential patients who were thought to have severe psychiatric problems (Shorter, 1997). After psychoanalysis, high functioning people became potential psychiatric patients, because, according to psychoanalytic ideology, these high functioning people actually had hidden neurotic problems that only trained psychoanalysts could detect. When psychoanalytic ideology began to take hold of American culture during the 1940s and 1950s, executives and housewives, who, during previous eras, would have never defined themselves as psychiatric patients, went to see psychiatrists in droves (Fancher, 1995). Suddenly, the people on Main Street had mental health problems.

During this golden era of psychoanalysis, psychiatrists were the only available psychotherapy practitioners. Psychiatrists successfully blocked competing professions from practicing psychoanalysis, and there were no viable alternative schools of psychotherapy (Fancher, 1995). However, this situation began to change during the 1950s when research psychologists, such as Hans Eysenck, openly criticized psychoanalysis. Indeed, Eysenck (1952) argued that the results of his research demonstrated that psychoanalysis was ineffective.

In addition to these critical attacks on psychoanalysis, competing schools of psychotherapy began to erode the foundation of psychiatric hegemony. Behaviorists, for instance, argued that psychology should be a strict science that is limited to observable phenomena, such as stimulus-response contingencies and behavioral emissions (Skinner, 1974). Because it was not observable or measurable, whatever happened in the black box of the mind was completely irrelevant, the behaviorists argued. Although academics, such as Watson (1919) and Skinner (1974), had been formulating behavioral ideology since the early part of the twentieth century, it was not until the mid-century that psychologists began to propose behavioral methods as mental health treatments. Wolpe (1958), for example, invented systematic desensitization to treat phobias. Wolpe claimed that he could rapidly cure phobias by inducing a relaxation response while progressively exposing clients to the phobic object or situation. It is easy to understand why these behavioral methods were attractive to mental health consumers, considering that the only other available treatment option was to see a psychoanalyst multiple times a week for many years.

Another competitor to psychoanalysis, psychological humanism, began to gain influence during the 1950s (DeCarvalho, 1990). The early humanists, such as Rogers (1957) and Maslow (1968), rejected behaviorism and psychoanalysis because of the reductionism inherent in these orientations (DeCarvalho, 1990). Psychoanalysis, humanists charged, reduced people to psychic structures, while behaviorism mechanically chopped clients into stimuli and behavioral responses (Matson, 1971). Appalled by this reductionism, humanists developed a "third-force" (DeCarvalho, 1990, p. 22) theory, which idealized client subjectivity and advocated genuine, holistic encounters between counselors and their clients. Rogers (1957) articulated the conditions of treatment for this new orientation, which involved unconditional positive regard, genuineness, and empathic responsiveness. Humanism, then, became a powerful force in mental health culture.

Behaviorism and humanism spawned additional competitors to psychoanalysis. Formal behaviorism, for example, gave way to cognitive approaches (e.g., Beck, 1976). Humanism, likewise, was an important precursor to a variety of treatment approaches, such as Gestalt therapy (Perls, 1969) and encounter groups (Elkins, 2009). As these new treatments became popular, nonmedical professionals were increasingly granted legal privileges to practice psychotherapy (Fancher, 1995). Meanwhile, the nonpsychoanalytic, biological psychiatrists, who had been the underdogs of the psychiatric profession, were gradually discovering effective pharmaceutical treatments for mental health problems (Shorter, 1997). Thus, the competition from alternative treatment approaches, and the rise of biological psychiatry, gradually undermined the dominance of psychoanalytic psychiatry.

The proliferation of new approaches to counseling resulted in a variety of divided schools of thought that were ideologically founded upon radically different assumptions about the causes of and treatments for mental health problems (Fancher, 1995). By the mid-1970s there were many, well-defined systems of psychotherapy, each of which had their own, relatively closed, communities of professional adherents. These orientations had completely different, often theoretically incompatible, answers to the question of what makes counseling effective. Indeed, as noted above, proponents from different schools of thought did not even agree on how to define effectiveness. Table 4.1 is a simplified summary of some of the basic assumptions of the more prominent schools of the time, all of which persist today.

Although admittedly an oversimplification, a simple scan of table 4.1 reveals the complete conceptual incompatibility of these dominant psychotherapy orientations in answering the question about what make counseling effective. For instance, the humanists and psychoanalysts idealize subjectivity, while the behaviorists think that it is completely irrelevant. The starting assumption of psychoanalysis is that people are essentially sexual and aggressive animals who repress their desires into the unconscious. Humanism,

Table 4.1. Basic Assumptions of Orientations to Counseling and Psychotherapy

Orientation	Cause of mental health problems	Treatment
Psycho-analysis	Unconscious conflict	Psychoanalyst interprets conflict to client
Behaviorism	Reinforcers and punishers in the environment cause and maintain symptoms	Behaviorist analyzes environmental contingencies and helps the client adjust them so that they are no longer supportive of maladaptive behaviors
Humanism	Natural drive to actualization was interrupted during development, which results in client incongruence	Humanistic therapist provides certain conditions of counseling (e.g., empathic responsiveness), which allows the natural process of growth to resume
Cognitive approaches	Irrational thoughts cause behavioral and emotional problems	Cognitive therapists help clients to transform maladaptive, irrational thoughts into adaptive, rational ones

alternatively, in stark contrast to psychoanalysis, presumes that people have a natural tendency toward growth and actualization, which is interrupted during development. Thoughts, according to the cognitivists, are the relevant source of clinical information, because cognitive approaches presume that irrational thinking is the cause of emotional and behavioral problems. It would be difficult to invent a more theoretically discordant set of premises. The theories started with completely different assumptions about human nature, which automatically led to diverse, theoretically incompatible answers to the question of what makes counseling effective.

As these schools of thought emerged and gained power during the 1960s and 1970s, they gained strong followings among academics and practitioners. Training institutes and graduate programs in mental health were usually oriented around one of these orientations (Fancher, 1995). This caused mental health culture to be composed of completely divided schools of thought, each of which had their own devoted adherents and professional infrastructure. This was an age of theoretical dogmatism during which the followers of one theory generally thought that the others were completely deluded about the causes and treatments for mental health problems. The psychoanalysts, for instance, presumed that other approaches merely brought about fleeting and superficial cures, while psychoanalysis resolved the underlying conflicts that were actually responsible for psychopathology. The behaviorists, who completely rejected the role of subjectivity in mental health treatment, in contrast, thought that the psychoanalysts based their interminable and self-serving treatment methods on a series of Freudian fairytales without any scientific evidence for doing so.

There were certainly new approaches to treatment proposed after the 1970s. Solution-focused (deShazer, 1985) and narrative approaches (White & Epston, 1990) to therapy, for example, were founded upon novel postmodernist assumptions, which will be discussed in a later chapter. A variety of new technical approaches, such as Eye Movement Desensitization Reprocessing (Shapiro, 1995), were also proposed. However, the basic four orientations (i.e., psychoanalysis, behaviorism, humanism, and cognitive approaches), and their theoretical offshoots, served as the foundation for mental health culture for decades to come. Once all of these orientations became strongly institutionalized as separate camps with their own adherents during the 1960s and 1970s, there was an urgent need to answer the question "what makes counseling effective?"

EMPIRICAL AND MULTICULTURAL FINDINGS

By the late 1970s, the effectiveness of counseling had been well established (Wampold, 2001). The fear that counseling worked no better than a placebo, which was inspired by the findings of critical researchers like Eyesynck (1952) in the 1950s, did not turn out to be true. Indeed, people clearly obtain tremendous benefits from participating in counseling (Seligman, 1995). The answer to the question "Is counseling effective?" then, was known to be "yes" by the end of the 1970s (Wampold, 2001).

Once this effectiveness question had been answered, a new question emerged: "Which method of counseling is the most effective?" Recall that, at the time this question was being posed, psychotherapy culture was divided into different schools of thought, each of which had fervent adherents who had devoted their professional lives to their favored orientation. To professionals in one camp, devotees of alternative orientations had completely missed the point. The intellectual infrastructure of the helping professions strongly resembled religious culture, with various groups of faithful followers worshipping and perpetuating their own beliefs (Fancher, 1995).

So, which group was correct about what makes counseling effective? Each orientation had academics, practitioners, and clients with a significant stake in the correctness of their favored perspective. Furthermore, the extant perspectives generally posited completely incompatible assumptions about the causes of and treatment for mental health problems. A statistical procedure known as meta-analysis provided a method for determining the winner.

Essentially, meta-analysis aggregates the effect sizes of multiple studies (Wampold, 2001). By the late 1970s, numerous research studies had been conducted on the various orientations to psychotherapy. With a meta-analysis, each of these studies could be assigned an effect size, which would statistically summarize the effectiveness of the orientation that had been investigated by the study. The meta-analytic procedures, then, could take all of the various effect sizes from each of the studies, aggregate them, and determine the winning school of psychotherapy. Presumably, this would answer the question "what makes counseling effective?"

By the late 1970s researchers were beginning to use meta-analytic methods to examine the differential outcomes of various psychotherapy orientations (Budd & Hughes, 2009). Surprisingly, meta-analyses revealed that all orientations work about the same (Smith & Glass, 1977). Generally speaking, none were significantly more effective than the others. Indeed, this equivalency finding has been consistent throughout decades of outcome research (Wampold, 2001).

Imagine the intellectual shock waves that this equivalency finding sent throughout the various schools of psychotherapy in the late 1970s and early 1980s. People had devoted their education, training, and professional lives to a particular treatment orientation. The fact that they all worked about the same was undoubtedly an incredibly difficult finding to digest. Some completely ignored the meta-analytic results. Others found ways to rationalize their continued adherence to their favored school of thought. Most notably, though, the finding that all approaches to treatment helped to about the same degree spawned a renewed interest in integrative and eclectic approaches to psychotherapy (Messer & Warren, 1995).

Instead of maintaining allegiance to a particular orientation, scholars could devote their energies to finding an optimal mixture of the various orientations. After all, if the various approaches to treatment were equally helpful, each of them must have something right. If the best elements of the various treatments could be combined, perhaps this would create a flexible, powerful, super approach to helping that would finally dissolve the embattled parochial culture of psychotherapy that had dominated previous eras.

There are various conceptual recipes for mixing the ingredients from different schools and baking them into an integrated, or eclectic, approach to psychotherapy. One recipe is that practitioners can simply use whatever techniques are effective with particular client problems without regard for theory. This approach is called *technical eclecticism* (Wampold, 2001). For the advocates of technical eclecticism (e.g., Beutler & Clarkin, 1990; Lazarus, 1981) the focus of psychotherapy should be to capitalize on whatever combination of techniques is known to be the most effective with particular client problems, without regard for the theoretical assumptions that gave rise to the techniques. For instance, for an adult client suffering from anxiety that is related to developmentally based conflicts with his father, perhaps relaxation exercises and the empty-chair technique (i.e., client could have a healing conversation with his father by pretending that his father was seated in an empty chair) could be employed. The fact that these techniques emerged from entirely different schools of thought (i.e., behavioral and Gestalt), which have virtually opposite assumptions about the cause of and cure for psychological problems, would not be of any concern to an advocate of technical eclecticism. Indeed, theories, for those advocating technical eclecticism, are meaningless distractions. Theories are only good insofar as they serve as the impetus for developing useful techniques. From this technical eclectic perspective, then, choosing the right combination of techniques is what makes counseling effective.

This minimization of theory for the sake of results initially sounds like a promising idea. However, cutting techniques out of their theoretical context and pasting them into some sort of therapeutic collage might reasonably change the power and effectiveness of the individual techniques (Messer & Warren, 1995). For example, if a psychoanalytic interpretation is offered to a client who has been in psychoanalytic therapy, the client has been indoctrinated into the assumptive world of psychoanalysis, which makes the interpretation reasonable, expected, and potentially helpful. In contrast, if a technically eclectic therapist suddenly tosses a psychoanalytic interpretation into a hodgepodge of other techniques, with no overarching conceptual orientation to give meaning to the techniques, the psychoanalytic interpretation might not only be ineffective, it might strike the client as completely bizarre.

In contrast to technical eclecticism, which minimizes the role of theory, the goal of *theoretical integration* is to combine various theories into an inclusive theory of human change (Wampold, 2001). If the finding that various orientations are equally effective is interpreted to mean that each theory has a piece of the truth, then it is reasonable to attempt to fashion a conceptual synthesis, which capitalizes on the theoretical insights of various approaches. This master theory could then spawn new techniques, which would be grounded in a strong and unified conceptual foundation. The idea behind what makes counseling effective in theoretical integration, then, is that each theory has a part of the truth about how to help people. If theories are combined in some internally consistent way, this would presumably lead to a powerful super theory that would contain multiple truths about effective counseling.

Theoretical integration has obvious limitations because the major theories of psychotherapy have radically different assumptions (Messer & Warren, 1995). Conceptual synthesis, then, often requires theoreticians to pound the round conceptual pegs of one theory into the square holes of another. Given this situation, a grand theory that unifies all of the conceptual elements of other theories is almost certainly an impossibility. Nevertheless, those who have promoted theoretical integration have proposed some novel conceptual combinations (e.g., Wachtel, 1977).

Those who advocate *common factors eclecticism* interpret the finding that there are no significant outcome differences in psychotherapy orientations to mean that the common factors of psychotherapy practice must be responsible for the therapeutic effect (Wampold, 2001). Unlike other types of eclecticism, the common factors approach does not emphasize commonalities in theory or techniques. Common factors theorists (e.g., Messer & Wampold, 2002) capitalize on commonalities in the treatment environment that therapists from various schools establish and maintain.

In this regard, if one were to observe a series of therapy sessions, conducted by therapists from different orientations, the activities of the therapists would almost certainly be very similar in spite of their theoretical differences. All of the therapists would probably listen intently, take a nonjudgmental stance, and attempt to understand their clients' point of view. Interventions that were based on the specifics of a particular orientation (e.g., cognitive reframing, psychoanalytic interpretation, etc.) would account for a very small, probably minuscule, portion of the therapy hours. Advocates of the common factors approach reasoned that it is the nonspecific factors (i.e., relational commonalities of all treatment approaches) that are responsible for therapeutic outcomes, not the specific techniques derived from particular theoretical orientations. The logic of common factors eclecticism has been fortified by the regular finding that the quality of the counseling relationship is the factor within the treatment that accounts for the largest proportion of the variance in outcomes (Lambert, 1992). That is, generally speaking, the better the relationship or treatment alliance between a counselor and a client, the better the treatment outcome, regardless of the theoretical orientation of the counselor or the techniques that are employed.

Is establishing a good relationship with clients all that there is to being an effective counselor, though? What other features of counseling might be important in determining good outcomes? To answer these questions, some theorists have extended common factors eclecticism by drawing from multicultural studies of healing (Frank & Frank, 1991; Torrey, 1972b). Instead of simply identifying the factors common to Western orientations to helping, these theorists aspired to learn the common factors of healing across cultures. Presumably, if cross-cultural patterns to healing could be identified, this could play a significant role in answering the question "what makes counseling effective?"

In this regard, Western psychotherapy is a fairly recent development that evolved in particular cultural contexts at a certain point in human history. Undoubtedly, psychotherapy contains the meanings and values of the historical/cultural context that gave rise to it. Determining the commonalities among healing approaches that exist across various cultures, though, might help to identify universal features that are common to all healing encounters. This would extend the theory of common factors eclecticism to encompass the common denominators of all healing, not just the relational factors of Western psychotherapy.

In fact, prior to the equivalency finding in psychotherapy, researchers had investigated common factors of healing across cultures. Torrey (1972b), for example, offered guidance about what psychotherapists could learn from witch doctors. As an anthropologist who later became a psychiatrist, Torrey went on various anthropological missions to study indigenous healing practices, hoping that Western psychotherapists might learn something from witch doctors. He, indeed, found multiple commonalities between witch doctors and psychotherapists.

The first commonality, which Torrey (1972b) called the "Principle of Rumpelstiltskin" (p. 70), is the act of naming and providing an explanation for a problem. For instance, a psychotherapist might inform a client that she has a diagnosis of depression, which is due to unresolved issues with her mother. The witch doctor, alternatively, might tell a tribal person that she is sick because "you have broken the taboo of your family. It has offended the sacred bear that protects your ancestors" (pp. 70–71). Both types of healers name the problem, which provides an immediate sense of relief to the person who came for help.

Torrey (1972b) also noted other commonalities between witch doctors and psychotherapists, such as the personal qualities of the healer. Although the personal qualities of the healer vary from culture to culture, these qualities seem to have something to do with the healing effect. Another commonality between witch doctors and psychotherapists (and probably all other healers) is that the healer raises the expectations of the sufferer. For instance, factors such as the dress and appearance of the healer (suit and tie or animal skins), decor of the meeting place (degrees or shrunken heads on the wall), and the training of the healer (graduate school or apprenticeship under a senior witch doctor) are designed to communicate that the healer is highly qualified, thereby raising the hopes and expectations of the sufferer.

Last, Torrey (1972b) found that both witch doctors and psychotherapists employ certain techniques to heal their clients. Surprisingly, Torrey concluded that there are strong commonalities among techniques across cultures. Both psychotherapists and witch doctors, for instance, use dream analysis as a helping technique. Indeed, Torrey concluded that the techniques used by psychotherapists are no more scientific than the techniques used by witch doctors. The idea that psychotherapeutic techniques are scientifically derived, then, is just a strategy used in Western culture to raise the hope and expectations of clients who live in a culture that places a high value on science (Frank & Frank, 1991; Hansen, 2002). Westerners are impressed by the value of science, just as tribal people might be impressed by the witch doctor's ability to connect with supernatural forces.

Torrey's (1972b) novel comparison of witch doctors and psychotherapists, then, revealed a host of surprising commonalities. Indeed, psychotherapy is probably just the Westernized version of a healing paradigm that is present across cultures. A cross-cultural investigation of healing, then, is a line of inquiry that has great promise to extend common factors eclecticism beyond Western psychotherapy to factors that are common in the healing paradigm throughout the world. If psychotherapists could capitalize on these universal common factors, perhaps the psychotherapeutic process could be strengthened and enriched.

The best articulation of these common factors of psychotherapy is Frank and Frank's (1991) outstanding book, *Persuasion and Healing*. I think that it should be required reading for all helping professionals. In this book, the authors synthesized the basic elements of all psychotherapies and outlined the commonalities between psychotherapy and culturally diverse healing situations, such as religious and magical forms of healing. The authors concluded that all psychotherapies have four common features, which also constitute diverse healing practices throughout the world.

First, psychotherapy involves an "emotionally charged, confiding relationship with a helping person" (Frank & Frank, 1991, p. 40). Second, psychotherapy takes place in "a healing setting" (p. 40). The setting is designed to communicate that the therapist has particular expertise, thereby raising the hopes of the client. In Western culture, this expertise is symbolized by a professional office setting where the accoutrement's of expertise, such as particular styles of dress, degrees, and licenses, are displayed. The setting also provides a sense of safety for the person coming for help.

Third, the psychotherapist offers "a rationale, conceptual scheme, or myth that provides a plausible explanation for the patient's symptoms and prescribes a ritual or procedure for resolving them" (Frank & Frank, 1991, p. 42). This is a commonality of all healing scenarios, including psychotherapy. The conceptual scheme of psychoanalysis, for instance, attributes symptoms to unconscious conflict. The cognitive rationale for symptoms, alternatively, is that they are the result of erroneous patterns of thought. Note that the healing rationale of psychotherapy only has to be plausible, not scientifically factual. Indeed, none of the narratives propounded by the various schools of psychotherapy have much scientific support (Hansen, 2002). Plausibility, of course, is a cultural phenomenon. What is plausible to a tribal person would be highly implausible to a Westerner and vice versa. Because Westerners generally find scientific explanations highly plausible, systems of psychotherapy are usually touted as being based on science, even though there is virtually no evidence that this is the case (Hansen, 2002).

Last, Frank and Frank (1991) maintain that a core feature of all psychotherapies is "a ritual or procedure that requires the active participation of both patient and therapist and that is believed by both to be the means of restoring the patient's health" (p. 43). The therapeutic bond is established and maintained by virtue of the ritual or procedures. Because both parties believe that it will be effective, the ritual or procedure is a powerful component of healing. The primary therapeutic procedure of psychoanalysis, for example, is for the patient to free associate and for the psychoanalyst to offer interpretations of the associations (Gabbard, 2010). Gradually, the patient comes to believe that the psychoanalyst has some special ability to accurately interpret the contents of his or her unconscious. This bonds the patient to the psychoanalyst, provides the participants with a shared, relationship strengthening activity, and inspires hope in the patient that the psychoanalyst has some special technical expertise that will eventually free him or her from psychological distress.

Frank and Frank (1991), then, took common factors eclecticism to its logical conclusion by examining the commonalities of all healing paradigms. They persuasively argued that counseling is just another instance of the implementation of certain seemingly universal contextual factors that have promoted healing throughout history in many diverse cultures. Wampold (2001), in his seminal book on outcomes in psychotherapy, aptly referred to Frank and Frank's model as the "contextual model" (p. 20) of psychotherapy. Wampold empirically compared the contextual model of psychotherapy to the medical model. In contrast to the contextual model, the medical model presumes that the application of specific techniques to particular mental disorders is responsible for positive outcomes. A comprehensive analysis of decades of treatment outcome studies not only demonstrated that the contextual model was the clear winner, but that "specific ingredients account for only 1% of the variance in outcomes" (Wampold, 2001, p. 204).

Therefore, helping professionals have some fairly clear beginning answers to the question "What makes counseling effective?" Clients gain the most benefit from factors that are common to all counseling orientations, such as the nonjudgmental stance of the counselor. These relational factors account for the majority of the within treatment outcome variance. In addition to the treatment alliance, it is important for counselors to ensure that certain contextual factors, which are a vital part of healing cross-culturally, are in place, such as a professional meeting place, an explanatory system, and associated rituals. For instance, the explanatory system of cognitive therapists is that thoughts cause emotional and behavioral difficulties. Cognitive rituals involve reframing and homework assignments to track negative thoughts. Psychoanalysts, alternatively, offer a narrative about unconscious processes to clients, along with accompanying rituals of free association and interpretation. These narrative, contextual factors promote healing, not anything intrinsic to the theoretical approach itself. In other words, an explanatory system and associated rituals provide an important context for effective counseling. The context, itself, is the healing force, and multiple helping orientations can be used to provide this context. Notably, it does not matter whether the explanatory system is objective or true (whatever that would mean); the only important issue is whether the new narrative offered by the counselor is persuasive to the client.

This contextual model helped me to make sense out of various observations that I formerly found troubling. For instance, at the agencies and clinics where I have worked, there have been some therapists who have had strong reputations for helping clients, and others who were mediocre or ineffective. Throughout the years, I have never been able to detect any correlation between the theoretical orientation of the therapist and the level of therapeutic effectiveness, which, of course, means that nothing intrinsic to a particular theory is responsible for effectiveness. While it was difficult for me to make sense of this observation early in my career, I now believe that the ability to establish a therapeutic relationship and the contextual factors of treatment form the basis for therapeutic effectiveness, regardless of theoretical orientation.

Indeed, early in my career, it was far more intellectually troubling for me to hear about clients who reported therapeutic benefit from meetings with ministers, astrologers, and fortune tellers than it was for me to observe the lack of correlation between the treatment orientation of mental health professionals and degree of effectiveness. With the contextual model, however, I now recognize that astrologers, for instance, have their own explanatory system and associated rituals that are designed to account for and alleviate human suffering. Generally speaking, astrology is not valued in our culture as a legitimate treatment intervention, which is the reason that few people would probably derive benefit from seeing an astrologer. However, the explanatory system and associated rituals that astrologers implement are consistent with the contextual model implemented by psychotherapists. Therefore, for the subset of people in our culture who place a high value on astrology, astrological treatment interventions would probably be very effective.

The contextual model allowed me to simultaneously value my training and appreciate diverse orientations to helping. In order to implement the contextual model, I needed to learn a theoretical orientation to implement with my clients. However, because it is the contextual factors of counseling that are responsible for effectiveness, there is nothing intrinsic to psychoanalysis, or any other orientation, that is responsible for positive outcomes, aside from the orientation being a plausible explanatory system to implement with clients. With the contextual model, I am now able to simultaneously value my training and appreciate diverse orientations to helping. I found my way out of the psychoanalytic labyrinth.

DISCUSSION AND CONCLUSIONS

In light of the findings about the factors that make counseling effective, the psychoanalytic professors in my graduate program were both right and wrong for their idealization and promotion of psychoanalysis. They were right because, as budding therapists, students should be required to master an explanatory system and associated rituals. If students are not taught a widely accepted orientation to counseling, they will not be able to function optimally as counselors because they will be missing a key element of the contextual model. Psychoanalysis is a rich explanatory system with multiple associated treatment rituals. However, my professors were wrong to imply that psychoanalysis was true, correct, or the best way to help people. There is abundant evidence that clients are helped by a variety of approaches to treatment, none of which, generally speaking, is more helpful than the others.

This equivalency finding also includes cognitive-behavioral approaches to treatment, which some erroneously think are proven to be more helpful than other orientations. Many of the research conclusions about the effectiveness of cognitive-behavioral treatments are simply byproducts of the research methodologies that were used to study treatment outcomes (Elkins, 2009; Wampold, 2001). Cognitive-behavioral therapies are one of the few treatments that can be reduced to step-by-step procedures (i.e., manualized), which is a necessity for the randomized control methodologies that were used to study treatment effectiveness in the 1990s (Leibert, 2012). However, limiting outcome research to treatments that are manualizable severely narrows the range of treatments that can be studied. This methodological side-effect led some to erroneously conclude that cognitive behavioral therapy was superior to other approaches. The consistent, meta-analytic findings, which span decades, however, unequivocally support the conclusion that no treatment orientation, generally speaking, is superior to others (Wampold, 2001).

In light of the contextual model and the findings that all treatment orientations, generally speaking, are equally effective, when I train students or supervisees, I try to balance the presentation of theoretical orientations with an attitude of humility about what the orientations can accomplish. This can be a difficult balance to strike because students often tend to idealize their favored approach. This idealization is probably the result of several factors: (a) Counseling is an ambiguous way to make a living. Client problems are usually complex, with no clear solutions. When thrust into this professional grey, a system of thought that purports to have black and white answers can be incredibly appealing, particularly to anxious, new professionals; (b) Mastering a theoretical orientation, especially one as complex as psychoanalysis, may require students to idealize the orientation. If I had not idealized psychoanalysis as the truth about human nature, I do not think that I would have devoted so many years to studying and practicing it; and (c) Students want to become experts who know the truth about how to help their future clients. It is difficult to rationalize the sacrifices that advanced training requires unless students are convinced that they are learning something true. All of these factors promote theoretical dogmatism.

Recognizing these educational dynamics, I teach my students and supervisees the basics of psychoanalytic theory and practice. However, after I have built up this system of thought, I knock it down by presenting the contextual model and the empirical findings about psychotherapy. My hope is that, by teaching the material in this manner, my students will acquire a beginning mastery of an explanatory system, but, at the same time, will avoid dogmatic adherence to a particular treatment approach. Ideally, then, I want my students and supervisees to gain the ability to think flexibly, reflectively, and critically about counseling practice, yet be prepared to offer sophisticated, healing explanatory systems, and associated rituals, to their clients.

I also want trainees to focus on the therapeutic relationship, which is a core part of the contextual model. To bring about this focus, I often ask my students and supervisees to engage in a reflective exercise, which has consistently proven to be very useful. Specifically, I ask them to recall a time when they felt psychologically distressed, went to someone for help (e.g., therapist, friend, spouse, minister, etc.), and left the interaction feeling a sense of relief. To protect their privacy, I deliberately tell them not to disclose the nature of their distress to me, but merely to tell me what the helper did to make them feel better. At this point, I ask that you, the reader, pause for a moment and engage in this reflective exercise.

I imagine that your responses to this exercise are about the same as the responses that my trainees have provided over the years. The helper is inevitably described as someone who listened intently, was not judgmental, validated and empathized with the experience of the distressed person, and, perhaps, after gently laying the relational groundwork, helped the person to see his or her distress from a new, helpful point of view. No one has ever reported that the helper implemented some technical procedure, corrected distorted cognitions, or rendered a diagnosis. Why, then, I ask my trainees, would you think that your clients would be helped by the types of responses that have never been helpful to you?

Ironically, for all that is known about the power of the therapeutic relationship and the contextual model, the far less effective medical model of psychotherapy has dominated mental health culture for decades (Hansen, 2005a, 2007d). Diagnostics, symptom based treatment planning, and other vestiges of medicalization have clearly overtaken modern psychotherapy practice. With all of the evidence against the medical model of psychotherapy, why has this vision of treatment become so dominant?

An obvious answer is that money, power, and prestige are associated with the medical model (Elkins, 2009). When psychotherapists began advocating for managed care reimbursement during the 1980s, they had to acquiesce to the demands of insurance companies to get paid. One of these demands was for helping professionals to use medical terminology to describe their practices, because the infrastructures of managed care companies were designed to provide reimbursement to health care professionals (i.e., surgeons, pediatricians, etc.). This economic situation caused psychotherapists to gradually adopt the medical model. Thus, to understand the odd twists and turns of the helping professions over the last several decades, just follow the money.

Furthermore, psychotherapists have achieved professional power and authority in contemporary culture by fooling the public (and themselves) into believing that they are quasi-medical, scientific professionals. If the truth were told (i.e., psychotherapy is fundamentally a relational profession that has nothing to do with medicine), the status, power, and income of helping professionals would be severely curtailed. In this regard, Flax (1990), a feminist psychoanalyst, offered the intriguing hypothesis that work, in contemporary Western culture, is defined according to prototypical masculine ways of being. To work means to penetrate and defeat problems, like a warrior engaged in combat. Surgery and the practice of law, for instance, are often described as heroic, masculine battles against an enemy. Alternatively, passive, feminine modes of engagement, such as caring for children, are generally not defined as work in modern society. This arbitrary, cultural devaluation of the feminine, according to Flax, has caused the helping professions to abandon their feminine, relational nature for the prestigious, but extremely ill-fitting, masculine ideals of science and medicine.

Fundamentally, though, counseling is conversational engineering. Counselors are experts at steering conversations in therapeutic directions. A warm relational environment, an explanatory system that is palatable to the client, and the implementation of particular contextual factors, which have been proven to promote healing across cultures throughout human history, are the fundamental, curative elements of the psychotherapeutic encounter. None of these factors can reasonably be described as medical. Also note that discovering some supposed truth about clients is completely irrelevant for effective helping to occur. How, though, could the truth possibly be irrelevant? The contextual model, then, led me to intriguing questions about truth, which are considered in the next two chapters.

Chapter Five

Are Truths Discovered or Created in the Counseling Relationship?

Imagine the following, fairly typical, exchange during a counseling session. A client says that he is upset because his boss does not like him. The client finds his work almost unbearable because of this situation. In the context of their ongoing psychodynamic treatment, the counselor draws a parallel between the boss and the client's father, suggesting that the boss, as a displaced representation of the father, is not really the problem at all. Suppose that, after hearing this interpretation, the client becomes sullen, starts to cry, and claims that he now recognizes that he had been superimposing the image of his father onto his boss, although he had not been aware that he had been doing so prior to the counselor pointing it out. In subsequent sessions, the client reports that the situation with his boss has improved substantially, a change that the client wholly attributes to the accuracy of the counselor's interpretation.

There are at least two ways to conceptualize this interaction. The first possibility is to assume that the counselor, by virtue of her training, accurately detected an enduring feature of the client's experience that the client had been unable to access. Advocates of this position might cite multiple points of evidence to support the assertion that the counselor had been correct: (a) the client agreed with the counselor's interpretation; (b) the insight brought about a deepening of the client's experience; and (c) the client's problem was substantially improved after the interpretation was offered. In short, the first perspective is that the counselor had discovered something real, objective, enduring, and true about the client.

The second perspective offers an entirely different conceptualization of this interaction. The counselor indoctrinated the client into a persuasive psychodynamic explanatory system. Within the theoretical parameters of this system, the participants created new narratives to account for the suffering of the client. The fact that one of these narratives helped the client substantially cannot be considered evidence that the counselor had discovered something true about the client. If sufferers were only helped when a truth about them had been discovered and revealed, then a variety of healing methods would have to be accepted as having the ability to uncover truths, including sorcery, astrology, and exorcism; these methods, and many others, have been helpful to sufferers. From this perspective, the counselor in the example simply offered a new, psychodynamic narrative to the client; the interpretation was an act of creation, not discovery.

Both of these perspectives are compelling. However, which one should counselors endorse? Can both be correct? If both are correct, how can counselors distinguish when they have accurately discovered something about a client versus when they have simply created a useful narrative? Does this distinction even matter? These are important questions to consider, particularly because traditional theories of counseling presume that healing depends on the ability of counselors to discover truths about their clients (Hansen, 2002).

A key assumption of traditional psychoanalytic theory, for instance, is that healing is dependent on the ability of therapists to make accurate inferences about the unconscious conflicts of their clients (Gabbard, 2010). Indeed, early psychoanalytic theorists drew a strong distinction between inexact and exact (i.e., true and accurate) interpretations (Glover, 1931). Cognitive healing is analogously dependent on the counselor's ability to accurately identify irrational patterns of thought (Ellis & Grieger, 1977). Through empathy, humanists aspire to objectively discover the contents of their clients' experiential universe (Rogers, 1957). In this regard, Rogers emphasized the importance of "*accurate*, empathic understanding" (italics added) (p. 99) as a necessary condition for personality change. Objective discovery of stimulus-response contingencies is the first step toward human change for behaviorists (Skinner, 1974). Note that all of these foundational theories depend upon a therapist's ability to accurately discover something about their clients (Hansen, 2002). The discovery of truth by psychotherapists sets clients free.

However, is it reasonable to suppose that counselors can ascertain truths about their clients? In a previous chapter, I briefly presented some of the communicative processes that must occur for language to be an adequate vehicle for conveying the truth about another person. These steps are worth elaborating in greater detail, as they are highly relevant to the issue of whether truths are discovered or created in the counseling encounter.

These steps can be organized according to a commonsensical breakdown of the processes within the counseling dyad that would allow counselors to discern the truth about their clients: First, some stable, enduring contents, which are waiting to be discovered, must reside in the mind of the client.

Depending on the theoretical orientation, these mental contents might be considered entirely conscious (i.e., humanism; Rogers, 1957), entirely unconscious (i.e., psychoanalysis; Gabbard, 2010), or consisting of stray experiential elements that had not been integrated into the client's cognitive frame of reference (i.e., cognitive-behaviorism; Mahoney, 1991). Second, in order to communicate with the counselor, the client must convert the experiences that surround these psychological elements into language. Third, the counselor processes what the client has said according to the counselor's personal psychology. Fourth, the counselor uses a theoretical orientation (or other means, such as intuition) to extract the actual truth about the client from what the client has said. If the counselor had accurately discovered a truth about the client, this extracted truth would match the original experiential content that had resided in the mind of the client (Hansen, 2004). For healing to occur (according to traditional theories of counseling), the therapist must share the discovered truth with the client, which entails two additional steps. In step five the counselor converts this extracted truth to language to speak to the client. Sixth, the client psychologically processes what the counselor said. The implementation of these steps is necessary for a counselor to accurately discern and communicate a truth about a client.

Note, however, that the assumptions inherent in these steps are highly problematic. For instance, the first step entails the assumption that the contents of the mind are stable and enduring. This assumption is highly questionable because memory research has clearly demonstrated that mental representations about the past shift and change as a function of the present and can even be wholly implanted (Loftus & Ketcham, 1994; Loftus & Pickrell, 1995). In light of this evidence, it is difficult to maintain the assumption that consistent, enduring mental contents are a foundational part of the mind. Furthermore, social constructionist theorists have persuasively argued that human beings are not closed, solipsistic containers of fixed mental representations, but engaged social actors whose experience changes as a function of the interactive milieu in which they participate (Gergen, 1999; McNamee, 1996). Memory research and social constructionist theorizing, then, have provided compelling evidence that the mind does not consist of stable, enduring representations that lie in wait to be objectively discovered by a properly trained helping professional.

Even if the first assumption could reasonably be endorsed, the idea that the nuances and complexities of human experience could be accurately encoded into the "arbitrary system of grunts and squeals" (Frederickson, 1999, p. 252) that humans call language (i.e., steps two and five), without any loss of the original experiential richness, seems incredibly naive (Spence, 1982). Consider the complex, layered, multi-faceted dimensions of any experience. Even a decision as simple as what to order for lunch takes place in a psychological matrix of associated experiences, memories, and multiple levels of personal meaning. When converted to the static symbols of language, the linguistic output (e.g., "I'll have a hamburger") could not possibly be an adequate representation of the totality of the experiences that gave rise to it.

To endorse steps three and six, it must be presumed that the personal psychology of the counselor and client has no impact on the processing of information. If the other assumptions are questionable, this assumption is outright laughable. Since Freud invented the constructs of transference (1912/1958b) and countertransference (1910/1957), it has become common knowledge that psychological factors have an enormous impact on information processing. Information that enters the mind is always transformed by personal biases, idiosyncratic meaning systems, and personality traits. Likewise, step four is problematic because there is no basis for assuming that theories are reliable guides to truth (Hansen, 2002). No theory has ever proven to be a psychological Rosetta Stone that is capable of translating the human communicative "system of grunts and squeals" (Frederickson, 1999, p. 252) into the richness of raw experience. Indeed, it is logically impossible for theories, as human, linguistic creations, to embody some hypothetical pristine truth because theories are epistemologically constrained by the language that constitutes them (the philosophical specifics of this problem are discussed below).

The assumption that counselors are capable of discovering truths about their clients, then, is highly problematic. However, if this truth assumption is abandoned entirely, a whole new set of problems and questions emerge. For instance, should counselors continue to use traditional theories of counseling, which are founded on the assumption that healing is dependent on the discovery of truths about clients? If clinical expertise is not defined by the ability to accurately discern truths about clients, what makes a clinician an expert? There are numerous additional problems associated with abandoning the idea of truth in the counseling encounter. Indeed, I have been preoccupied with them for many years.

PERSONAL AND PROFESSIONAL
SIGNIFICANCE OF THE QUESTION

My struggles with the truth issue in counseling probably began in graduate school. My psychoanalytic professors taught me that everyone creates their own universe. After all, people cannot crawl outside of their minds to see what the world is like beyond their perceptions. All stimuli from the outside world that enter our sensory organs must travel through, and necessarily be transformed by, our preexisting mental web of meanings. When listening to case material the gurus would capitalize on this assumption to infer the unique meaning systems that the client had unconsciously superimposed onto the transference, contemporary relationships, and other areas of life. It was all very compelling to me.

Although the general idea of psychic meaning creation is fairly common among traditional psychoanalysts, some of my professors inflated this idea to the point where it threatened to logically blowup and theoretically destroy the entire therapeutic enterprise. The reason that this isolated mind assumption was so prevalent in my graduate training had more to do with intellectual genealogy than clinical observation, empirical evidence, or theoretical logic. Specifically, one of the most influential professors in my program had spent a significant amount of his training under the tutelage of the psychoanalytic psychiatrist John Dorsey.

I have never met John Dorsey, so everything that I report about him is based on stories that I heard from my former professor. Dorsey was psychoanalyzed by Sigmund Freud, which elevated everything that he said to a prophetic level. Somewhere during the course of his training, Dorsey took the isolated mind assumption to its logical extreme and decided to incorporate it into his day to day life. Reportedly, upon encountering someone, Dorsey's standard greeting was "how is my you today?" He was not joking. If the world is an individual, psychic creation, then the qualities that are attributed to others are a byproduct of one's own psyche, which would make the customary greeting of "how are you today?" a logically erroneous salutation. Sometimes it was difficult to keep from bursting out laughing when my professor described the many ways that Dorsey had incorporated his strange, theoretically derived interpersonal style into his life.

I found the psychoanalytic take on the isolated mind idea compelling (but not compelling enough to act like Dorsey). However, after this idea had intellectually stewed in my mind for a while, I began to contemplate a disturbing question. One day, I decided to ask one of my psychoanalytic professors the question, which, by that point, had been bothering me for weeks. I raised my hand, and the interaction went something like the following. I said "Patients get better when the true contents of their unconscious are discovered by a therapist and interpreted to them." Professor Solipsist (not his real name) agreed. "However, the therapist and patient each create their own psychological universes, right?" I asked. The guru agreed that they do, and I continued my questioning. "If both parties are inescapably encased in their own psychic worlds, then, by definition, one party can never know the pure, unbiased truth about the other. Logically, this means that the psychoanalytic interpretations formulated by a therapist can never be true, objective representations of a patient's psychology. How, then, can patients ever change if change is dependent on the truth of the interpretations?" Professor Solipsist paused briefly but did not flinch. "Very slowly," he said with a strong air of sagacity. "That is why therapy takes so long."

Of course this answer is complete gibberish. At first, I tried to take it seriously. I wondered whether he meant that the walls of the psyche could eventually be broken down and the pristine truth about the other could finally burst through. He could not have possibly meant this, though. That would have undermined the entire edifice of his theory. I did not know how to resolve this problem, and, not being philosophers, my professors were of no help to me. They just sailed ahead in the psychoanalytic ship seemingly oblivious to the gaping logical hole in the hull. But, referring back to the central question of this chapter, how can therapists ever discover anything true about their clients if all perceptions of clients are necessarily created within the minds of therapists? All conclusions about clients, then, must be therapist creations, not objective discoveries. To get on with my studies, I tried to ignore the problem, but it came up for me again, in a different form, after I became a professor.

As a professor, I eventually became convinced that the contextual model of treatment offered the best understanding of the factors that helped clients in the counseling process. As discussed in the previous chapter, this model presumes that certain contextual factors of therapy, such as the therapeutic relationship, explanatory systems, and associated rituals, are responsible for positive therapeutic outcomes, not the truth value of what the counselor says to the client (Frank & Frank, 1991; Wampold, 2001). Retrospectively, I regarded psychoanalytic treatment as potentially helpful, not because it was true (whatever that would mean), but because it provided a useful context for conducting treatment. By accepting the contextual model, I was able to easily shed the problem of how truth could be communicated between two isolated minds that had bedeviled me during graduate school. Truth no longer mattered. However, abandoning the ideal of truth gave me a whole new set of questions and problems.

In this regard, I was familiar with the basic, philosophical assumptions that supported the pursuit of truth. Essentially, these assumptions are that by employing objective, scientific observation, humankind can gain incremental increases in knowledge, and, thereby, become better masters of the forces of nature (Anderson, 1990; Rosenau, 1992). Human progress is dependent on the gradual acquisition of truth. These assumptions had been so baked into my education (and, indeed, Western culture) that I had never thought to question them. My old professors proceeded from this epistemological model, which is probably the reason that their ideas seemed so natural and compelling to me. However, because I endorsed the contextual model, which completely trivialized the ideal of truth, I concomitantly felt obliged to abandon the philosophical assumptions that made the acquisition of truth a reasonable goal. With the contextual model, discovery of truth no longer mattered; created narratives were the key to healing. However, the abandonment of truth created an enormous sinkhole in my intellect that I was eager to fill in. At the level of practice, I was perfectly comfortable with trading creation for discovery. At a deeper, philosophical level, though, I was intellectually disturbed by the idea that the goal of discovering the truth, a pursuit that I had idealized for decades, could simply be dropped like a bad habit.

Was there, I wondered, a system of thought that supported the abandonment of truth? Could I replace my old philosophical assumptions about truth with a system that rejected it? Would these new assumptions help me to understand whether truths are discovered or created in counseling? My scholarly course for the foreseeable future was set.

Frankly, I am not sure if the question of whether truths are discovered or created in the counseling process is important for practicing counselors to consider. I think that the question can be meaningful and interesting, but I know many fine practitioners who have never given it any thought. However, a thorough consideration of the question might open up new intellectual and practical possibilities for counselors that they would not have considered if the question had not been posed. This has certainly been the case for me.

ARE TRUTHS DISCOVERED OR CREATED IN THE COUNSELING RELATIONSHIP?

To appreciate the ideal of truth and its associated critiques as they relate to the counseling relationship, the historical and philosophical development of truth as a goal of inquiry must be considered. By design, my presentation of this matter is abbreviated, but it should provide the reader with a general overview of the important issues.

Truth and Modernism

The Western ideal of truth was arguably first articulated by the philosopher Plato over two thousand years ago. Plato posited that the objects and ideas of the world are actually imperfect representations of objects and ideas that exist in an ideal world of forms (Plato, 1968). For instance, there are many examples of chairs in the world. However, according to Plato, there must be some perfect ideal of "chairness" that unites all of these instances of chairs. Similarly, abstract concepts like justice and beauty have perfect representations in the world of forms. Plato, therefore, posited a difference between mere appearances and the perfect, essential reality from which these imperfect appearances are derived. The goal of philosophical investigation, then, is to ascertain the essential forms. This goal of discovering the real truth, which lurks behind mere appearances, set the stage for philosophical investigation for thousands of years (Whitehead, 1979).

Plato (1968) represented these concepts about truth in his allegory of the cave. Plato asked readers to imagine a group of people who had been chained and rendered immobile since an early time in their lives. These people face a cave wall, and there is a large fire burning behind them. When something passes between the fire and their backs, the cave dwellers only see the shadow of whatever passes on the cave wall. Because they have been facing the wall for so many years, they mistake the appearance of the shadow for the real object. Philosophical reasoning, Plato argued, has the power to unshackle people, turn them around, and cause them to see the essential object that is casting the shadow, so that people will not mistake the appearance of the shadow for the essential reality that is casting it.

Note that this is the model of knowing that traditional approaches to counseling employ (Hansen, 2002). Traditional psychoanalysts, for example, presume that there is an unconscious truth that lurks behind the mere conscious shadows of client reports. Likewise, behaviorists and cognitive-behaviorists search for the stimulus-response contingencies and irrational patterns of thinking that represent the true essence of their clients' problems. In this sense, traditional therapists are like philosophers who work in Plato's cave to unshackle their clients, turn them around, and make them face the truth about themselves. From this Platonic perspective, psychotherapy is about discovery, not creation. The idea of truth did not end with Plato, though. Truth, and associated ideals, received a renewed emphasis centuries later, during the Enlightenment.

The Enlightenment was a period of fervent intellectual activity that began in Europe at about the middle of the seventeenth century (Hicks, 2004). Enlightenment philosophers, such as Descartes, Bacon, and Locke, emphasized reason as the key to knowledge and human progress (Hicks, 2004). For instance, Descartes (1988), in his six meditations, began by doubting everything that he had ever been taught, including the existence of others and himself. By employing this radical doubt, Descartes thought that he could clear away all of his incorrect beliefs, start fresh, and build up a true, accurate philosophical system based on pure reason. Descartes' method of systematic reasoning, and his philosophical conclusions about existence, mind-body dualism, and other matters, has had a lasting impact on Western culture (Hicks, 2004).

This Enlightenment emphasis on reason naturally gave rise to an idealization of individualism and science (Hicks, 2004). Individuals engage in reasoning, so highlighting the role of the individual was a natural by-product of Enlightenment thought. Likewise, science was also idealized as a method of systematic, practical reasoning to find truths about the world. This Enlightenment narrative, which emphasized reason, individualism, and science as the keys to human progress, is referred to as *modernism* (Hansen, 2004).

Modernist assumptions shaped the formation of Western culture, which is strongly individualistic and places a high value on scientific truths (Tarnas, 1991). Traditional orientations to psychotherapy adopted these modernist ideals (Hansen, 2002). Psychoanalysis, behaviorism, cognitive-behaviorism, and humanism, for example, all begin with the assumption that problems and their resolutions lie within individuals. This modernist assumption of individualism, however, is completely arbitrary. Problems could easily be thought of as residing in families, institutions, societies, cultures, and so on. The fact that all of the foundational systems of psychotherapy presumed the centrality of the individual is evidence of the tremendous influence of modernist ideals on the psychotherapeutic enterprise (Gergen, 1999; Hansen, 2002).

The other side of modernism, the search for truth through scientific objectivity, is also an intrinsic component of traditional schools of psychotherapy (Hansen, 2002). Freud, for instance, considered himself a scientist who objectively discovered truths about the unconscious (Gay, 1988). By employing particular conditions of treatment, such as abstinence, anonymity, and neutrality, Freud thought that psychoanalysts could become neutral, scientific observers who discover objective truths about their clients (Gabbard, 2005). Subsequent systems of psychotherapy followed this modernist model by also employing pseudo-scientific directives designed to ensure therapeutic objectivity (Hansen, 2002, 2006b). For all traditional counseling orientations, then, healing is about discovery, not creation.

Postmodernism

Even though they had a tremendous influence on Western culture generally, and schools of psychotherapy in particular, the basic assumptions of modernism were subjected to philosophical critiques in the centuries that followed the Enlightenment. The eighteenth-century German philosopher Immanuel Kant (2007), for instance, argued that attributions about reality are shaped by individual minds. According to Kant, the mind structures reality, not the other way around (Hicks, 2004).

Likewise, the Enlightenment ideal of the individual self also began to crack under the weight of subsequent ideological critiques. As a primary example, Freud posited that individuals are determined by a part of their mind that is completely inaccessible to them (Rorty, 1986). Therefore, after Freud, it became difficult to "remain faithful to the common-sense assumption that a single human body typically contains a single self" (Rorty, 1986, p. 4). Like the connection between reason and truth, then, the modernist idea of a willful, consolidated, conscious self that is at the center of human action was subject to various critiques during the centuries that followed the Enlightenment (Hicks, 2004; Rosenau, 1992).

During the twentieth century, these critiques of modernism began to coalesce into a new movement, which is called *postmodernism* (Hansen, 2004). Twentieth-century philosophers such as Lyotard (1984), Derrrida (1995),

Foucault (1980), and Rorty (1979), systematically deconstructed the modernist project (Chessick, 1996). The ideas of these philosophers are frequently complex, obscure, and they often disagree with each other. However, there are various core assumptions that arguably form the foundation of the postmodernist critique of modernism. For instance, the idea that humans can acquire objective knowledge of the true Platonic essences of objects and ideals has been thoroughly critiqued by postmodernists on at least three grounds. These postmodernist critiques have direct implications for the issue of whether counselors discover or create truths about their clients.

First, different people and communities have different perspectives on concepts and objects. Consider a ball, for example. One person might regard the ball as an object with which to play; another might belong to a community (e.g., chemist, engineer, physicist, etc.) that is interested in some particular physical property of the ball; an artist, as another example, might consider the ball an aesthetic object. Who is correct about the true essence of the ball? Because there are a potentially infinite number of justifiable ways to perceive the objects of the world, the Platonic ideal of one, true essence is difficult (if not impossible) to maintain. This line of reasoning has resulted in some postmodernist philosophers endorsing an *anti-essentialist* position, which, in direct contrast to Platonic essentialism, maintains that it is logically indefensible to think of objects and concepts as having true, singular essences (Muran, 2001). With this critique in mind, is it reasonable for counselors to set out to find some true, objective essence about their clients?

Indeed, according to Kuhn (1996), science does not even have the ability to draw objective conclusions about the nature of reality. Scientists are members of communities, Kuhn argued, which indoctrinate participants into standards about the proper questions to ask and the acceptable answers. For example, a researcher who is investigating the neurochemical basis of depression will surely not conclude that depression is caused by psychological, subatomic, economic, or relational factors. The scientific community to which the researcher belongs would not accept those types of conclusions. Therefore, science can never be purely objective. Science is simply a tool to help communities of scientists solve whatever problems happen to concern them. However, there is no reason to suppose that the human puzzles that particular communities are devoted to solving have any connection to the supposed intrinsic nature of reality. If it is untenable to think that scientists make pure, objective discoveries about tangible, physical phenomena, how can it possibly be reasonable to assume that counselors make objective discoveries about the intangible, psychic phenomena of their clients?

A second critique of the concept of essential truth is based on the fact that human beings rely exclusively on language to encode ideas and communicate (Rorty, 1999). Language is a human creation, of course, because the objects of the world do not name themselves. People superimpose the categories inherent in their linguistic system onto the world (Baudrillard, 1995). Because all truth claims must be expressed in language, and language is a human construction, all truth claims must also be a human construction (Rorty, 1989). There is no way to get outside of language to determine if a truth claim corresponds with some hypothetical reality beyond linguistic constructions (Rorty, 1999). Indeed, any attempt to formulate such a correspondence would also have to be described in language, thereby automatically entrapping the description in a linguistic, epistemological prison. This idea of being trapped by language is an important philosophical critique of the concept of objective truth. Derrida (1995) summarized this problem when he stated that "there is nothing outside of the text" (p. 89).

As an illustrative example of this linguistic critique, consider, as an analogy to language, a roadmap that is used by a driver to find a destination. This map, which depicts roads and cities, is obviously not equivalent to the territory that it describes. Indeed, a different type of map might be structured according to rock formations, historical monuments, oil reserves, or the locations of a particular species of plant. There are probably an infinite number of maps that could be made to describe the same territory. What, though, does the actual territory consist of beyond any map or mental way of depicting it? Just as it is impossible to conceive of some objective territory beyond human maps or categories, it is analogously impossible to know supposed objective realities beyond human ways of linguistically describing them. Language is a human-made map that determines how the stuff of the world is perceived (Baudrillard, 1995). In this regard, because all orientations to helping clients, by definition, are linguistic constructions, is it reasonable to presume that any orientation to counseling is capable of objectively depicting the psychological phenomena that it describes? If this linguistic critique is endorsed, psychological theories create perceptions of clients, just like maps create perceptions of territories (Baudrillard, 1995). Some of these perceptions may indeed be useful. However, according to postmodernists, it is logically erroneous to suppose that certain ways of linguistically describing the world are closer to the true territory of the world than others (Rorty, 1999). This linguistic critique completely undermines the notion that the language used by psychotherapists could ever represent discovered, precisely correspondent phenomena about clients. Conclusions derived in the counseling scenario are always trapped in the language that is used to describe them, thereby making objective discovery a logically indefensible goal in the helping professions.

The third critique, like the second, is also fundamentally linguistic, but it draws from a Darwinian perspective. From an evolutionary point of view language evolved because it aided the survival of the human species (Dennett, 1995). Language, therefore, is fundamentally a tool that humans used successfully to cope with the environment, just like the wheel, microprocessor, and color vision. It would be absurd to presume, however, that tools for coping with reality could somehow transform into media for copying it (Hansen, 2008; Rorty, 1999). A fork, for example, is a tool for coping with the task of eating. The presumption that the fork could somehow transform into a tool that embodied the singular, true essence of eating would be ridiculous. By extension, it is also absurd to presume that language, as a tool for coping, could transform into media for copying the true essence of reality. Language, therefore, cannot embody truth (i.e., a copy of true reality) because language, from an evolutionary perspective, is merely a tool for coping (Rorty, 1999). By extension, psychological theories, as linguistic constructions, can never copy (i.e., embody a correspondent truth) the essence of psychological phenomena; they are only tools for coping with client problems. Likewise, all linguistic exchanges that occur within the counseling scenario are coping tools, not correspondent copies of the psychological phenomena that the parties are attempting to communicate. This tool view of language completely undermines the assumption that the language of counselors is capable of representing discoveries about clients.

Of course, these critiques of truth have implications for the other side of the Enlightenment coin, the idealization of individualism or self. Specifically, if the search for foundational essence to the world is logically misguided, then it is also erroneous to think of the self as having a foundational essence (Rosenau, 1992). The self, and the various properties that have been attributed to it, are linguistic creations (just like all other meanings attributed to the world). From the postmodernist perspective, selves are created, not discovered. It might be useful for therapists to talk about a client finding his or her true self, but, on a philosophical level, there is no basis for reifying the idea of self as having some special ontological status that sets it apart from other linguistic entities that humans have created.

There are at least two clarifications to these postmodernist critiques of truth and self that are important to note. First, postmodernists, generally speaking, do not deny the existence of reality (Rorty, 1999). There is certainly stuff in the world. However, this stuff does not have any meaning until humans ascribe meaning to it in the form of language. Language does not bring reality into being—it just organizes and categorizes the stuff of the universe according to human perceptions and needs. Second, the postmodernists have generally not claimed that their system of thought is true, objective, or accurate (Rorty, 1989). Indeed, this would be a hypocritical claim for them to make. They have simply suggested that the modernist project has run its course, and that a postmodernist vantage point might bring about some new, interesting, and potentially useful possibilities.

These postmodernist assumptions have, indeed, caused some ideological shifts in counseling research, practice, and theorizing over the past several decades. Qualitative researchers, for instance, reject the quantitative research goal of discovering universal laws of reality through objective, scientific investigation (Berg, 2004). Rather than reducing phenomena to numbers, qualitative researchers aim to understand unreduced human meaning systems as they emerge in local environments. At the level of practice, new therapeutic systems have been inspired by postmodernist ideology. Solution-focused therapists, for instance, focus on creating solutions rather than discovering the source of problems (deShazer, 1985). As another example from counseling practice, narrative therapists have developed multiple techniques, such as externalizing symptoms, which are derived from viewing the therapeutic scenario as a place where realities are created, not discovered (White & Epston, 1990). These professional trends are united by their rejection of the idea that the goal of inquiry should be the discovery of some objective, universal reality.

Theoretically, postmodernist assumptions theoretically align with the constructivist and social constructionist movements in the social sciences. Constructivism presumes that individuals are closed, biological entities who create meaning systems (Hansen, 2004). Although this assumption of individual meaning creation is somewhat consistent with postmodernist philosophy, the constructivist idea that humans operate in individual, closed systems was eventually regarded by many as an unsuitable foundation upon which to build orientations to human helping (Rudes & Guterman, 2007). During the 1980s, counseling theorists began to turn to social constructionism, an ideological position that is also built on a postmodernist foundation (Rudes & Guterman, 2007).

Social constructionism has had a tremendous influence on the helping professions. Essentially, social constructionism posits that groups create realities (Hansen, 2004). Therefore, according to social constructionists, behavior can be best understood through a social lens, not an individual one. In this regard, Gergen (1999), arguably the most influential proponent of the social constructionist position, noted that words only acquire meaning in the context of social interaction. People play coordinated, social language games, such as the culturally prescribed rules for greeting someone. If a person were to suddenly utter the phrase "good morning" during the middle of an argument, Gergen noted, this would be seen as bizarre, because the greeting would have occurred outside of a justifiable social context. Therefore, according to social constructionists, human meaning and intention can be best understood from a social vantage point, not from the traditional individual perspective.

In keeping with their social epistemology, social constructionists do not conceive of the self as an enduring, interiorized property of individuals. Rather, multiple selves are continually created and transformed, as a function of the group in which a person participates (Gergen, 1995; McNamee, 1996). For instance, I regularly play the roles of father, husband, professor, and clinical consultant. According to social constructionists, there is no reason to unify these various roles under the banner of a cohesive, internal self. Selves are created and transformed by various identity possibilities that originate in social communities. Indeed, Gergen (1995) argued, the singular, unified self of modernism is an outmoded and maladaptive ideal. The psychologically healthy person wears multiple self-masks, which allow for flexible adaptations to various relational circumstances.

As social constructionist assumptions gained wider attention, some helping professionals began to discard the model of therapeutic discovery and to conceive of the meanings that emerge in the therapeutic relationship as joint creations between the counselor and client. For instance, this conceptualization of mutual influence between counselors and clients in psychoanalysis is often referred to as a two-person psychology, which is in contrast to the one-person psychology that dominated psychoanalytic thought for most of the twentieth century (Gill, 1994). Indeed, the acceptance of social constructionism as a system for understanding the psychotherapeutic process has led some psychoanalytic theorists to speak of "cotransference" (Orange, 1995, p. 63), instead of transference or countertransference, in recognition of the socially constructed, co-created nature of any phenomena that emerges in the helping encounter (Hoffman, 1998). For social constructionists, then, meanings are socially created in the counseling situation, not discovered within the client by a perspicacious counselor (Hansen, 2004).

Postmodernist ideology sheds new light on the questions raised about the clinical vignette at the beginning of this chapter. With the postmodernist critique, it is difficult to maintain the position that the therapist discovered something accurate, objectively true, and enduring about the client when the therapist suggested that the client had superimposed the image of his father onto the boss. Indeed, perhaps the distinction between discovery and creation in the counseling situation is irrelevant, given that clients are often helped by counseling interventions regardless of whether these interventions are regarded as embodying some discovered truth. However, for me, a positive side effect of conceptualizing the activities of the counselor as acts of creation rather than discovery is that I have become more flexible in my practice. Because I no longer worry about uncovering the truth about the people I try to help, I do not allow myself to be dogmatically tied to particular treatment methods that are designed to uncover the truth. This attitudinal change about my work, and the flexible type of practice that I am now able to bring to clients, trainees, and supervisees, was well worth the effort it took me to consider the discovery versus creation question.

DISCUSSION AND CONCLUSIONS

If one is persuaded by the postmodernist critique, it is difficult to continue to endorse the idea that counselors discover something true about their clients. Abandoning the idea of discovery in favor of creation, however, portends some interesting consequences and challenges for the helping professions. For instance, should traditional orientations to counseling be abandoned because they are based on the logically problematic ideal of discovery?

I believe that traditional orientations can be retained, despite their questionable epistemological foundation. The truth value of counseling orientations does not seem to have anything to do with healing (Frank & Frank, 1991). Traditional theoretical storylines and rituals can have tremendous persuasive appeal to clients, thereby making them potentially very useful in the counseling process (Hansen, 2002). In this regard, I do not believe that students should be taught that theories are representations of truth. Idealizing theories as embodiments of truth encourages students to become dogmatically locked into particular perspectives at an early point in their career. As a professor and supervisor, I prefer to present theories as narrative possibilities to be used in the service of helping clients. The fundamental task of education in the helping professions, then, is familiarize students with healing narratives and associated rituals, so that students can learn various ways to transform the life stories of their clients, which have generated suffering, into hopeful, optimistic narratives that promote growth and healing (Hansen, 2006a).

Indeed, perhaps the best resolution to the discovery versus creation question might be to completely forget about the distinction between discovery and creation within the counseling process. Perhaps it is a waste of time to fret over a theoretical distinction if it does not make a practical difference (Rorty, 1982). In this regard, I have suggested that counselors design their interventions to have "experiential resonance" (Hansen, 2005b, p. 10). The concept of experiential resonance sidesteps the discovery versus creation debate, while acknowledging that counselors should intervene in ways that are meaningful to their clients. Even if truth and discovery are rejected on a philosophical level, it does not mean that these concepts should be rejected on the level of experience. Counseling narratives should feel true to clients. Otherwise, they are unlikely to work. Truth is still a good experiential target, even though it might be a bad philosophical one.

What are the consequences, though, of abandoning truth altogether as an intellectual organizing principle in the helping professions? The postmodernists have offered compelling reasons to eliminate the role of truth as a central factor in professional discourse. What might replace truth, though? Can the profession survive without it? Truth has been the professional compass in the helping professions for the past century. What might guide us now, if truth is no longer an option? These, and related questions, are considered in the next chapter.

Chapter Six

Should Counselors Abandon
the Idea of Truth?

This last question may strike readers as a radical one to ask. The pursuit of truth has been the hallmark of intellectual culture for thousands of years (Tarnas, 1991). Specifically, there are several assumptions about truth that are strongly ingrained in the Western mindset: (a) the material phenomena of the universe is beholden to enduring truths or laws of nature; (b) when proper methods are employed, these truths can be objectively known by human beings; and (c) human progress is dependent upon the acquisition of these truths (Anderson, 1990). For instance, there are certain truths about the causes of and cures for diseases. If these truths are discovered, humans can achieve mastery over nature, alleviate the suffering caused by disease, and gradually progress to a more utopian, disease-free existence.

As mentioned in the previous chapter, traditional orientations to counseling were founded on these Western assumptions about truth and progress (Hansen, 2002). Psychoanalysts, for instance, presumed that counselors, by employing certain methods, could discover the true, unconscious conflicts of their clients (Gabbard, 2010). By helping clients face repressed truths, counselors could bring about healing. Other traditional counseling theories employed this same "truth will set you free" strategy, just with different conceptual spins. Whether counselors are theoretically charged with discovering cognitions, stimulus-response contingencies, or the unreduced contents of consciousness, the following epistemological formula is part of the theoretical DNA of traditional counseling orientations: (a) expert counselors, by employing particular, theoretically derived methods, discover truths about their clients; (b) these discovered truths are shared with clients; and (c) client betterment is a function of the degree to which clients psychologically utilize these truths (Hansen, 2002). If counselors abandon truth, they would be discarding a construct that has been the foundation of the helping professions since their inception.

Before addressing the monumental question of whether truth should be abandoned, however, it is important to define truth in a philosophically precise way. According to philosophers, there are multiple ways to conceptualize truth (Schmitt, 1995). For instance, the coherence theory of truth maintains that a belief must be consistent with a larger, coherent system of beliefs in order for it to be true (Schmitt, 1995). A review of the various theories of truth is beyond the scope of this discussion. However, the type of truth that is being considered in this chapter is the correspondence theory of truth. Whenever I critique the concept of truth in this chapter, I am specifically referring to the correspondence theory of truth.

The correspondence theory is a definition of truth that is consistent with the way that most people think about truth. In short, beliefs or statements are true if they correspond to the intrinsic nature of reality (Schmitt, 1995). For example, the belief that the flu is caused by a virus is considered true because it presumably matches the objective reality about the flu. The statement that "elephants can fly," alternatively, is not considered true because it presumably does not align with the intrinsic nature of elephants. Similarly, as applied to the counseling situation, a statement about a client is true if the statement corresponds to some intrinsic truth about the client. For instance, if a counselor told a client that "your anger protects you from experiencing grief," this statement would be true, according to the correspondence theory, if the statement was a match for the intrinsic nature of the client's experience. The idea of truth has been subject to multiple philosophical critiques, which were discussed in the previous chapter. However, these critiques are worth reviewing as they apply to the correspondence theory of truth. First, people have diverse perceptions of reality, which are a function of their individual and communal meaning systems (Hansen, 2002, 2004). Various people might view a cow, for instance, as livestock to be sold, as a pet, as a sacred animal, as a collection of subatomic particles that is mostly empty space, or as a physiological system of organs to be studied. Which view corresponds to the intrinsic nature of the cow? Indeed, to determine which beliefs or statements are most correspondent to the intrinsic nature of reality, both the statement and the intrinsic nature of reality must be known, so the degree to which they match can be determined. However, given that the intrinsic nature of reality is not known, how can the degree of correspondence between human beliefs and intrinsic reality ever be assessed? In short, it is impossible to tell if two things correspond if one of them cannot be seen (Rorty, 2000b).

Second, all beliefs are encoded in language. Humans invent language and superimpose linguistic categories onto the stuff of the universe (Rorty, 1999). Therefore, as a human-created superimposition, language can never correspond to the essence of reality (Hansen, 2007a; Rorty, 1999). It is impossible to get outside of language to determine if human linguistic categories correspond to the supposed way that reality actually is beyond these categories. Third, also related to language, is the Darwinist critique. The ability to communicate with language was naturally selected for as a coping tool because it helped human animals to adapt and thrive (Dennett, 1995). However, language can never *copy* reality (i.e., directly correspond to it), because language, like all other adaptive tools that evolved through natural selection, can only *cope* with reality (Hansen, 2008; Rorty, 2000a). Therefore, language, because it is a tool, can never be correspondent with the intrinsic nature of reality, any more than a fork, as a tool, can be correspondent with the intrinsic nature of eating.

Philosophically, then, the idea that statements and beliefs can be assessed according to their relative proximity to the intrinsic nature of reality (i.e., correspondence theory of truth) has been thoroughly critiqued, particularly by postmodernist philosophers. Indeed, if one is persuaded by these critiques, it is impossible to maintain the assumption that a counselor's conceptualization of a client's problem or experience can ever be true, in the sense of directly corresponding to some actual, essential truth about the client (Hansen, 2007a). However, even if one is not persuaded by these philosophical critiques, there are other compelling practical reasons to abandon the idea of truth.

Foucault (1980), a twentieth-century French philosopher, equated truth with power. To understand his reasoning, consider that any truth claim also represents an implicit judgment about what is not true. For instance, the contention that a heterosexual orientation is the true sign of psychological and moral health automatically relegates alternative orientations to an inferior, nontrue status. Even the most casual glance at human history will reveal the numerous ways, throughout millennia, that the truth claim of one group has caused the disenfranchisement and suffering of another. Indeed, the helping professions arguably have a long history of using truth claims to the detriment of mental health consumers.

In this regard, Masson, in his fascinating book *Against Therapy* (1994), argued that all psychotherapy is inherently harmful because of the omnipresent power differential between therapist and client. To make his case, Masson provided detailed accounts of the surprisingly nefarious activities of many of the icons of the helping professions, including Freud, Jung, Perls, and Rosen. Although disturbing, the book is a real eye-opener, and an excellent treatise on the ways in which power can corrupt the helping process. Masson does not cite truth as the culprit. However, it is easy to infer that many of the incidents of abuse described in his book had their foundations in truth claims that were made by influential professionals, who then used the claims as instruments of power to take advantage of clients.

The author who has best elaborated the power dynamics behind common mental health practices, however, is arguably Thomas Szasz, whose many books detail the ways in which psychiatric ideology has deprived individuals of freedom. Szasz's (1961) critique began with the intriguing and provocative argument that mental illness is a myth. Physical illnesses, Szasz argued, are always diagnosed on the basis of a deviation from normative physical functioning. For instance, anyone, regardless of culture or period of human history, who has a body temperature of 104 degrees is very ill because this temperature represents a significant deviation from the normal temperature of the human body. By extension, the concept of mental illness, to be logically justifiable, must also be defined by a deviation from normative functioning. The construct of illness cannot exist without a definition of normality. Unlike the normative constants that allow for definitions of physical illness, however, there are no stable, universal, culture-free definitions of normal psychological functioning. Indeed, even within the United States, the definition of normalcy has changed radically over the decades. Homosexuality, for instance was considered a psychiatric illness before 1973 (Shorter, 1997). As another example, *drapetomania* was the psychiatric diagnosis given to runaway slaves, who, according to the definition of normalcy at the time, must have surely been ill to flee the civilized lives that their benevolent masters had provided for them (Shorter, 1997).

Szasz (1961), therefore, concluded that mental illness must be a myth because there are no unwavering baseline definitions of psychological normalcy from which to derive the concept of mental illness. Because definitions of psychological normalcy continually shift and change, the designation of mental illness is nothing more than a social judgment about what a society finds deviant at a particular point in history. Furthermore, illness is something that occurs to a tangible body. Mental illness, then, in addition to being logically unfounded, is an oxymoron, because illness, as a material concept, cannot be attributed to the immaterial realm of the mind. In this regard, I had the opportunity to meet Dr. Szasz, who, incidentally, is the only one of my conference table geniuses (see introductory chapter) that I have met. During our talk, he argued that the idea of *mental illness* was as oxymoronic as the phrase *married bachelor*. Both phrases are inherently contradictory.

Because mental illness is a logical absurdity on multiple levels, Szasz (1961) reasoned, psychiatrists are never justified in using this mythical construct to deprive patients of their liberty (i.e., hospitalizing them against their will). The titles of Szasz's many books, such as *Psychiatry: The Science of Lies* (2008), *Psychiatric Slavery* (1977), and *Cruel Compassion: Psychiatric Control of Society's Unwanted* (1994), betray his conclusions about so-called psychiatric "truth" and the ways in which the erroneous concept of mental illness is used to control vulnerable members of society. Szasz (who, notably, is a psychiatrist), then, has authored a significant body of work that convincingly details the ways in which so-called truth has been used for the purpose of power in the mental health realm.

Therefore, truth is not only logically problematic on a philosophical level; truth has also been used frequently as a destructive instrument of power throughout history generally and within the helping professions in particular. Given this analysis, perhaps counselors should abandon truth altogether. However, in addition to simply getting rid of problems, there might be some additional benefits to abandoning truth.

Rorty (1991), for instance, proposed that abandoning the ideal of truth can result in increased solidarity. If one seeks contact with some objective truth that exists beyond humanity, then one will be less inclined to value engagement with fellow human beings. In other words, looking skyward (for truth), diminishes opportunities to look around (at others). Rorty (1991) said it best:

> Insofar as she seeks objectivity, she distances herself from the actual persons around her not by thinking of herself as a member of some other real or imaginary group, but rather by attaching herself to something which can be described without reference to any particular human beings (p. 21)

In short, the desire for objectivity lessens the desire for solidarity. Rorty's abstract, philosophical thesis has practical implications for the practice of counseling.

If Rorty's (1991) philosophical ideas are imported into the counseling realm, it means that the more counselors are attached to a supposedly true theory, the less they will be in genuine relational contact with their clients (Hansen, 2007c). This is a vital point to consider, given that practitioners, throughout the history of the helping professions, often became dogmatically tied to particular theoretical orientations (Fancher, 1995). Mid-century psychoanalysts, for example, frequently conducted multi-year treatments with clients even though there were credible empirical challenges about the efficacy of their treatment methods (Eysenck, 1952). With Rorty's critique in mind, these psychoanalysts were probably more devoted to their favored theory than to their clients.

Abandoning truth, then, may promote egalitarianism in the counseling relationship, allow counselors to be more flexible and less dogmatic, and encourage the parties in the counseling dyad to focus on the meanings created within their relationship, rather than on the external, prepackaged explanations offered by supposedly true theories (Hansen, 2007a). Indeed, there are many compelling philosophical and practical reasons for counselors to abandon the idea of truth.

However, if counselors abandon truth, they will have a new set of challenging questions with which to contend. For instance, counselors have traditionally justified their interventions on the basis of truth (Hansen, 2002), arguing, for example, that cognitive reframing is the proper treatment intervention for a particular client because irrational thoughts are the true cause of depression. Psychoanalysts, as another example, drew a distinction between inexact versus exact (i.e., true) interpretations (Glover, 1931). However, if counselors abandon truth, how will counselors know how to help their clients? What will take the place of truth to justify interventions in the counseling relationship?

In this regard, what would stop counselors from saying anything to clients if truth no longer mattered? A client could be told that she was depressed because aliens had invaded her body. Anxiety could be explained as a gravitational phenomenon that was brought about by having too much iron in one's diet. Without truth, what would stop counselors from saying such things? Indeed, what would happen to ethics and the professional parameters of the counseling relationship? Without truth as a guide, what would stop counselors from borrowing money from or sleeping with their clients? Clearly, then, counselors cannot just abandon truth without some sort of suitable replacement to structure their professional lives.

PERSONAL AND PROFESSIONAL
SIGNIFICANCE OF THE QUESTION

I pursued higher education because (among other reasons) I wanted to know the truth about what made people tick. As I mentioned in previous chapters, I became mesmerized by the psychoanalytic explanatory model, which, like some kind of freaky oracle, seemed to have an answer for every question I posed. Moreover, the answers were always deep, rich, and satisfying. The theory was a perfect match for my intellectual disposition, and the more I learned, the more I was drawn in. My professors, who were also enamored by psychoanalysis, promoted the idea that Freud and his followers had found the truth. Although I had many questions when I left graduate school, I was confident that I was traveling down the right theoretical path.

However, my naively secure vision of truth was shattered by the realization that multiple orientations help people equally well. How could this be? The true theory should do a better job of helping people than the false ones, I reasoned. After a period of intellectual struggles based on my disillusionment with psychoanalysis, I eventually started to take advantage of the freedom afforded to me by my new professorial position and began to entertain philosophical critiques of truth. These critiques, many of which I presented at the beginning of this chapter, opened my eyes to a radical, new thought: truth, as a philosophically unsupportable and practically damaging construct, is not a suitable goal of inquiry (Rorty, 1998). Although I was completely astonished and intrigued by this novel idea, certain elements of my history made it a frightening idea to accept.

In my late teens, friends told me about the types of college majors that they were planning to pursue, such as accounting, pre-law, and education. I remember thinking that they were all going to study rules, regulations, and practices that human beings had invented. I wanted to pursue knowledge beyond human invention—to get to the real truth and not simply become a part of an institution that people had created. This was an important part of my internal justification for becoming a psychology major. It was a vital justification for me to hang on to because I was frequently questioned about my reasons for pursuing a major (i.e., psychology) that often had little practical payoff. Indeed, the noble pursuit of truth continued to supply me with the motivation necessary to get through the long haul of graduate school while, in my financially unstable state, I watched my friends and younger brothers obtain well-paying jobs, buy homes, and start their lives with a strong financial base.

If I abandoned the idea of truth, however, I would be forced to admit that psychology was simply another institutionalized set of concepts and practices that was created by humans, not some higher, truth-based calling. While there were clearly advantages to abandoning the idea of truth, the absence of truth made me feel like my intellectual pursuits had been cheap, hollow, and false, instead of having been nobly above the career goals of my peers. So, for me, there was an emotional tie to truth, not just an intellectual one.

In the end, I decided to follow the philosophers who had persuaded me that truth was not a suitable goal of inquiry. Once I had a secure job in academia, I no longer needed a noble justification for enduring the sacrifices of graduate school. The fundamentally narcissistic function that truth had served for me was now unnecessary and could be exchanged for the pure joy of intellectual discovery that the gift of academic freedom made possible.

Once I had worked through my emotional conflicts about the abandonment of truth, I could see the incredible potential of giving up on the idea that beliefs and statements should be sorted according to their degree of correspondence with some intrinsic reality. Psychotherapy systems that had once seemed completely incompatible could now be integrated as narratives about the human condition (Hansen, 2002). For purposes of theoretical integration, it no longer mattered that psychoanalysis presumed that unconscious conflict was at the root of psychological problems, while cognitivism blamed irrational thoughts and humanism cited incongruence as the culprit. If all of these theories were considered true, it would almost certainly be impossible to integrate them because of their irresolvable conceptual incompatibilities. Without truth, however, these theories could become unified as various stories about the human condition. I had not learned the truth in graduate school;

I had simply learned an intriguing and sophisticated narrative about the human condition.

Abandoning truth, then, helped me to finally find my way out of the psychoanalytic labyrinth. I could now accept, and experiment with, multiple orientations without worrying about truth. Furthermore, I found my new epistemological stance highly congruent with the insights I was acquiring from *Persuasion and Healing* (Frank & Frank, 1991), which is almost certainly the book that has had the most influence on my thinking about the counseling situation. As discussed in a previous chapter, the authors engaged in a multicultural analysis of healing and concluded that counseling is simply another instance of a healing paradigm that occurs universally across diverse cultures. Specifically, a societally-sanctioned expert heals demoralized sufferers by proffering culturally accepted, healing narratives and associated rituals. Truth has nothing to do with this contextual model of healing. With Frank and Frank (1991), Wampold (2001), and the postmodernists (e.g., Rorty, 1999), my conceptual trifecta was complete: (a) theoretical: the contextual model of healing; (b) empirical: Wampold's meta-analytic findings, which strongly supported the contextual model; and (c) philosophical: logical justifications (provided by postmodernism) for the minimization of truth in the contextual model

I finally felt like I was standing on solid theoretical ground. Throughout my intellectual struggles with psychoanalysis, I knew what I wanted the end product to be: I wanted to value psychoanalysis and not think that I had wasted my time and money in graduate school, but, at the same time, I also wanted to flexibly accept other systems of thought. Initially, I had no idea how to theoretically achieve this goal. However, with my new conceptual trifecta, I could still value psychoanalysis as a valuable healing narrative with associated rituals (that I could have only mastered by the extensive training that I endured in graduate school) but also accept and experiment with alternative orientations to helping. I was exuberant.

It was not long before the intellectual honeymoon was over, though. Indeed, abandoning truth seemed to create as many problems as it solved. Essentially, if truth is abandoned, what alternative criterion could be used to guide professional activities? I was not comfortable with a restricted, dogmatic profession, but I certainly did not want an "anything goes" profession, either.

Although I struggled with the idea of truth on a personal level, I also think that it is important for helping professionals to consider questions about truth and whether truth should be abandoned. On any given day numerous clients are informed about their irrational thoughts, diagnostic status, the true meanings of their symptoms, the way that their childhood is connected to their adult life, and numerous other weighty, deeply personal conclusions about their lives. What basis do counselors have for saying any of these things? Is it because they are true? How do counselors know that they are true? What could serve as evidence? If they are not considered true, what is the justification for choosing one intervention over another? These questions should certainly not be taken lightly. Clients often take what their counselors say to heart. One sentence uttered by a counselor might change the way that a client thinks about him or herself for life.

Truth claims also have a longstanding tradition of being used in the service of power (Foucault, 1980). If a counselor regards the things that he or she says to a client as true, this automatically has implications for the dynamics of power within the counseling relationship. Specifically, with truth, the counselor is in the role of an informed authority or expert, which automatically relegates the status of the client to a hapless sufferer who is dependent on the expertise of the counselor. As discussed earlier in this chapter, this relational dynamic has been associated with horrendous abuses, both in human history generally and within the counseling situation specifically. Readers may think that they would never propagate such abuses, even within the truth paradigm. However, power can be insidious and subtle. Clients can be subtly used to support the self-esteem of counselors, as social outlets, and to make counselors feel better about their own troubled lives, for example. There are numerous nuanced and hidden ways that counselors can unconsciously use their power to operate beneath the surface of the manifest counseling process to get their needs met. Indeed, neither the counselor nor the client may recognize them. A careful analysis of clinical processes, though, often reveals the hidden ways that well-intentioned counselors subtly and unconsciously use clients for selfish, emotional purposes. Truth is the gateway to the power that corrupts.

If taken seriously, this analysis of truth places the helping professions in a tremendous quandary. On the one hand, truth is philosophically unsupportable and automatically creates a potentially harmful power dynamic within the counseling situation. On the other hand, truth has traditionally been the guide to professional action. Should counselors abandon truth? If so, what might replace it? Possible resolutions to this conflict are presented in the next section.

SHOULD COUNSELORS ABANDON THE IDEA OF TRUTH?

The answer to the question of whether counselors should abandon the idea of truth is arguably dependent on whether there is a suitable replacement for truth to guide professional action. A truth-based profession may be unacceptable, but so is a rudderless one. Indeed, I think that truth can be replaced by a superior professional compass. To appreciate my proposal, it is important to understand the different varieties of philosophers who have critiqued the idea

of truth. While these postmodernist philosophers have commonalities, particularly their rejection of the Enlightenment association between truth, knowledge, and human progress, there are some important differences.

In this regard, Rosenau (1992) usefully divided postmodernists into skeptical and affirmative camps. Skeptical postmodernist philosophers (e.g., Derrida, 1995) thoroughly deconstruct truth, self, and other foundations of Western thought. However, these pessimistic, skeptical philosophers do not offer
anything to replace these foundations; they simply destroy without rebuild-
ing. This radical deconstruction may be acceptable for some fields, such as
literary analysis, which is exclusively concerned with texts, not people. However, Rosenau argued, this skeptical postmodernism is not suitable for the
social sciences, which rely heavily on constructs like the self. In contrast to
the skeptics, the affirmative postmodernists, while also critical of modernism, offer a more hopeful vision and argue that, even without truth, there are
criteria for making some value choices over others.

Similar to Rosenau, Polkinghorne (1992) divided postmodernists into two
groups: affirmative and relativist. Both varieties, Polkinghorne argued, share
three ideological themes: (1) foundationlessness, (2) fragmentariness, and (3)
constructivism. Foundationlessness is a logical by-product of the fact that
people can never escape their perceptions to discover a true reality beyond
those perceptions. Because this perceptual trap is an inherent part of the
human condition, it is impossible for any human endeavor to be built upon
foundational knowledge (i.e., knowledge beyond human perceptions). Fragmentariness means that human explanatory systems (because they tend to be
framed in terms of universal conclusions) inevitably smooth over reality,
which postmodernists conceptualize as local and fragmented rather than universal and cohesive. Last, constructivism, consistent with the general postmodernist view, means that "human knowledge is a construction built from
the cognitive processes . . . and embodied interactions with the world of
material objects, others and self" (Polkinghorne, 1992, p. 150). This emphasis on foundationlessness, fragmentariness, and constructivism, Polkinghorne
argued, can be found, at least to some extent, in all postmodernist philosophical systems.

If simply left with these three themes, there would be no basis for making
one choice over the other. By extinguishing the guiding light of truth, the
relativist postmodernists have eliminated the compass that has traditionally
guided human knowledge and progress. Moreover, these philosophers have
not concerned themselves with finding a replacement for truth that might
alleviate this problem of relativism. Indeed, relativist postmodernists, after
demolishing the foundations of Western thought, seem content to simply
play in the rubble.

In contrast, affirmative postmodernists, while adopting the first three
themes, also incorporate neopragmatism (Polkinghorne, 1992). With neo-

pragmatism, affirmative postmodernist philosophers (e.g., Rorty, 1999) add an ideological element for guiding human actions that the relativist postmodernists do not provide. In order to understand neopragmatism, and how it is used to circumvent the problem of relativism, the basic assumptions of pragmatism must be understood.

Pragmatism is a uniquely American school of philosophical thought. During the late nineteenth and early twentieth centuries, James, Dewey, and Peirce emerged as the chief proponents of pragmatism (Menand, 2001). While these philosophers disagreed on many of the finer points, the unifying theme of pragmatism is that "an idea is true, so long as to believe it is profitable to our lives" (James, 1995, p. 30). The definition of truth for pragmatists, then, is not whether a belief corresponds to the intrinsic nature of reality, but whether the belief is useful (Rorty, 1999). To illustrate their point, earlier in this chapter I noted that the belief that the flu is caused by a virus is ordinarily considered true, while the belief that elephants can fly is regarded as false. As an illustration of the logic of pragmatism, the reason that the latter belief should be considered false is simply because no one has found a use for it, not because it fails to correspond with the intrinsic nature of reality (whatever that would mean). Attributing the flu to a virus, alternatively, has been an incredibly useful belief for the medical community to adopt.

It may seem bizarre to think that a belief in flying elephants would be regarded as untrue simply because no one has found a use for it. However, imagine how people in the fifteenth century would have regarded the belief that material objects consist mostly of empty space. This belief would have been regarded as completely bizarre and untrue, perhaps even more so than a belief in flying elephants would be today. Remarkably, however, the community of modern physicists has made incredible advances by endorsing this belief. Beliefs, then, according to pragmatists, should be judged exclusively by their practical payoff (Rorty, 1999). As far as I know, a belief in flying elephants does not advance the interests of any contemporary community. However, this belief (or other beliefs that seem bizarre today) might be considered true in the future if people find a use for it.

To put pragmatism in a historical context, pragmatist philosophers were strongly influenced by Darwin, who proposed his theory of evolution shortly before the emergence of the pragmatist movement (Menand, 2001). The fundamental thesis of the theory of evolution is that organisms adapt to the environment through the process of natural selection (Dennett, 1995). Beavers build dams, for instance, because natural selection favored the survival of beavers who had acquired this adaptational trait. It would be absurd to ask whether beavers approximate the intrinsic nature of reality when they build dams. Dam building is simply an adaptational coping strategy. Analogously, pragmatists regard belief systems as adaptational coping strategies that are used by human animals. Therefore, it is similarly absurd to ask whether belief systems are correspondent with the intrinsic nature of reality. Beliefs are simply adaptational tools like beaver dams. It makes no sense to judge any tool according to its ability to copy the intrinsic nature of reality (Hansen, 2008; Rorty, 2000a). The test of a belief, then, just like the test of any tool, is the degree to which it fosters adaptation or the advancement of human interests.

During the mid-twentieth century, pragmatism fell out of favor with mainstream philosophy. However, during the 1970s, Rorty (1979) revived pragmatism and integrated it into postmodernist thought. This new postmodernist form of pragmatism is called *neopragmatism* (Polkinghorne, 1992; Rorty, 1999). Neopragmatism differs from traditional pragmatism in that neopragmatic philosophers, unlike the earlier pragmatists, generally endorsed the three themes of postmodernist discourse that were outlined by Polkinghorne (1992) (i.e., foundationlessness, fragmentariness, and constructivism). Furthermore, neopragmatism, in keeping with many movements in twentieth-century philosophy, placed a strong emphasis on language (Rorty, 1999).

By incorporating neopragmatism into postmodernist thought, the affirmative postmodernists were able to reject the correspondence theory of truth while avoiding the conceptual pitfalls of their relativist counterparts (Polkinghorne, 1992). Neopragmatism provides a criterion for determining whether a belief should be endorsed: whether the belief is useful. Of course, judgments about whether a belief is useful vary across communities and over historical eras. A useful belief to a chemist is probably useless to a poet and vice versa. Likewise, many of the beliefs of people who lived during the 1800s are probably relatively useless today, just as many of beliefs of today will have likely outlived their usefulness in the coming decades.

The essential point of neopragmatism, though, is that human progress should not be defined by progressive approximations to the intrinsic nature of reality. Rather, progress is dependent upon learning the lessons of history, avoiding mistakes that were made in the past, and coming together to dialogue about what the best course of action would be in a particular situation. Open-minded dialogue, ideological flexibility, and human solidarity are the engines that drive humanity forward, not attempts to determine whether human beliefs match the supposed eternal laws of the universe (i.e., correspondence theory of truth) (Rorty, 1999).

I was thrilled to discover neopragmatism. With the affirmative postmodernists, I could reject the correspondence theory of truth while retaining a basis for making decisions. As applied to counseling, my theoretical trifecta now had a fourth element: (1) Frank & Frank's (1991) contextual model of healing; (2) Wampold's (2001) empirical support for the contextual model; (3) philosophical justifications (provided by postmodernism) for the minimization of truth in the contextual model; and (4) a basis for making decisions without truth (i.e., neopragmatism) (Hansen, 2007a; Rorty, 1999).

Truth and Justification

This philosophical overview of postmodernism and neopragmatism has been fairly abstract. Neopragmatism, however, has numerous concrete implications for the counseling process and the helping professions. To illustrate these implications, it is useful to consider the neopragmatic distinction between truth and justification. This truth/justification distinction is simply another way of saying that the correspondence theory of truth should be replaced by good reasons (i.e., justifications) for making choices. However, the truth/justification distinction helps to position abstract neopragmatic thought into the concrete realm of the helping professions.

To illustrate the truth/justification distinction, if practicing counselors were asked why they chose to respond to a client in a particular way, most would probably offer reasons for their interventions, such as the belief that it would help relieve the client's emotional suffering, was consistent with the client's worldview, or that it would strengthen the counseling relationship. Some counselors might make the additional claim that they chose their response because it reflected a truth about the client that the client would benefit from knowing. Reasons for selecting counseling interventions, then, can be sorted into two broad categories: (1) practical justifications and (2) truth.

However, if contemporary philosophical critiques of truth are taken seriously, truth cannot possibly serve as a reason for choosing counseling interventions because the correspondence theory of truth is logically indefensible. Without truth, though, counselors would only have the neopragmatic criterion of practical justification to serve as the guide for choosing counseling interventions. Is it reasonable for counselors to use justification alone as a guide for responding to clients? What would be the advantages (or possible disadvantages) of eliminating truth altogether as a basis for action? Philosophers in the pragmatist tradition cite at least two logical arguments for replacing truth with justification, which are related to the reasons for abandoning the ideal of truth that were discussed earlier in this chapter. In the context of the truth/justification distinction, however, these reasons can be directly tied to counseling practice.

First, justifications are recognizable; truth is not (Rorty, 2000b). That is, justifications (i.e., reasons for actions) can be publicly discussed, debated, and communicated to others. In contrast, the supposed intrinsic nature of reality (i.e., truth) is inherently unrecognizable; there are no criteria to determine if someone has accurately identified it. Therefore, helping professionals should rely exclusively on justifications, not truth, for professional decision making, because it is nonsensical to aim for a target (i.e., truth) that cannot be seen (Rorty, 2000b). In this regard, decisions about whether clinical interventions are justifiable (i.e., whether there are good reasons for them or whether other interventions should be considered) can be discussed and debated with clients, colleagues, and supervisors. However, there is no way to evaluate whether a clinical intervention is a good match for the intrinsic nature of some element of client reality.

Second, truth adds nothing to justification alone; truth makes no difference about what to do (Rorty, 1998). To illustrate, suppose a counselor is considering one of two interventions to use with a client. There are multiple good reasons (i.e., justifications) for choosing the first intervention, such as the intervention has been helpful to the client in the past, there is research evidence supporting its effectiveness with this client's condition, and the counselor has training in the use of this intervention. Alternatively, there is no basis for choosing the second intervention. Should the additional claim that one or the other of these interventions is true make a difference about which intervention the counselor selects? The counselor has a solid basis for choosing the first intervention, regardless of whether it is considered representative of some truth. On the other hand, if truth is attributed to the second intervention, there is still no good reason for selecting it. Truth, therefore, adds no value to the criterion of justification because it makes no difference to action. Because it adds no value, pragmatist philosophers argue that truth should be eliminated as a criterion for action and wholly replaced by justification (Rorty, 1998). Instead of operating within an epistemological ecosystem that is structured by truth, then, this critique implies that counselors should choose to structure their clinical decision making according to justifications alone; truth claims do not provide any additive value.

In addition to these abstract, philosophical arguments for replacing truth with justification, helping professionals can achieve multiple practical benefits by giving up the idea of discovered truth and relying on justifications alone. Some of these benefits have been mentioned previously. However, they take on new professional meanings when couched within the truth/ justification distinction.

First, training in particular theories can sometimes promote dogmatic allegiance to a single system of thought (Fancher, 1995; Frank & Frank, 1991). Although contemporary practitioners are far more eclectic than their counterparts from decades ago (when training often involved a thorough indoctrination in a particular theory; Fancher, 1995), counselors are still at risk for idealizing their favorite theories. The idea that certain theories are true (coupled with the natural professional insecurity of counselors in training who often want to find the "correct" theory) often promotes idealization of theories and subsequent dogmatism. If theories are not considered true, but simply deemed justifiable tools to use with particular clients at certain times, there is no reason to maintain an allegiance to a particular theory. The attitude that theories do not represent truths can promote flexible practice, rather than rigid adherence to interventions derived from a favored theory. Substituting truth for justification, then, can help counselors maintain an allegiance to the betterment of their clients, rather than to systems of thought (Hansen, 2007a).

Second, as mentioned previously, truth claims often promote oppression. Human history is riddled with accounts of people using truth claims to dominate, disempower, and oppress others (Foucalt, 1980). Indeed, mental health practitioners are alarmingly susceptible to using truth claims to control and manipulate their clients (Masson, 1994; Parker, 2007). If counselors endorse a model of justification, and give up the idea that they possess truths that their clients lack, perhaps counselors would engage in fewer subtle (and overt) power plays at the expense of their clients. Another important reason for counselors to replace truth with justification, then, is so that abuses of power might be minimized in the counseling relationship.

A third practical benefit of replacing truth with justification is greater appreciation for diversity. The caseload of helping professionals often includes clients with diverse worldviews and belief systems. Rather than judge these client characteristics in terms of how well they align with some supposed truth, the criterion of justification allows counselors to appreciate diverse client perspectives. For example, within a truth paradigm, a counselor might view clients who have a strong belief in astrology in a negative psychological light, if the counselor does not deem astrological beliefs to be representative of truth. However, if only concerned with justification, the same counselor, rather than judging the belief in accordance to its congruence with the intrinsic nature of reality, would appreciate, and be deeply interested in, a client's reasons for maintaining a belief in astrology and the practical consequences of that belief for the client. Trading truth for justification helps counselors trade judgment for appreciation.

Last, justifications continually evolve, while truth, once "found," often prevents further options from being considered (Rorty, 1989). Truth claims are the ultimate conversation stoppers. Mid-century psychoanalysts, for example, recommended psychoanalytic treatment for clients, even as briefer, more effective treatment options for mental health problems began to emerge (Fancher, 1995; Shorter, 1997). Aside from the self-serving nature of this recommendation, psychoanalytic education (particularly during the mid-century) strongly promoted the idea that psychoanalytic postulates about human nature were undeniably true (Kirsner, 2000). After being trained in the psychoanalytic truth, it was unthinkable for psychoanalysts to consider that a theory based on completely opposite premises (e.g., behaviorism) could be helpful.

Therefore, truth, by definition, inhibits the further exploration of ideas, options, and professional actions. Ideally, counselors should always be searching for new and better ways to help their clients. Using justification as the sole basis for action encourages counselors to debate reasons for engaging in particular actions, discuss these reasons with colleagues and clients, and come to conclusions through critical dialogue. In contrast, truth, when used as a basis for action, is a conversation stopper. Once a counselor believes that the truth about a client has been found, this attitude tends to close down further discussion. Truth claims are the surest way to discourage potentially generative professional dialogue.

Justifications alone, then, can arguably provide a sufficient basis for guiding professional actions in the helping professions. Furthermore, trading truth for justification promotes ongoing dialogue, sensitizes professionals to abuses of power, and encourages the continual evolution of ideas. Therefore, there is no need to endorse the problem-ridden ideal of static, discovered truth when a neopragmatic model of dynamic, flexible, and evolving justifications can serve as a superior foundation for practice in the helping professions.

DISCUSSION AND CONCLUSIONS

There are multiple, compelling reasons to answer the question "Should counselors abandon the idea of truth?" in the affirmative. I have argued that the correspondence theory of truth is an inherently flawed construct, from both a logical, philosophical perspective and from the vantage point of the dynamic epistemological interplay within the counseling relationship. Counselors can provide necessary and sufficient justifications for their interventions without appealing to the problem-ridden idea of truth. As an illustration of this point, if a counselor claimed that an intervention was chosen because it was consistent with the role and ethics of the counselor, congruent with the subjective experience and worldview of the client, and was anticipated to be helpful to the client, the additional claim that the intervention also embodied the truth would be a useless and potentially harmful addendum, which would add nothing to the justifications alone, except to bog them down with epistemological nonsense and damaging dynamics of power. I am not claiming, however, that an emphasis on justification represents a correct or true vision of reality. This would be a hypocritical claim to make within an epistemology that rejects the correspondence theory of truth. I am simply making the case, like others (e.g., Rorty, 1998), that there are troubling negative consequences to endorsing the modernist, truth paradigm. The neopragmatic emphasis on justification, in my estimation, brings positive consequences to the helping encounter that are not readily available within the modernist system of thought.

It is also important to note that I am not arguing that objective truth exists and that humans are simply incapable of discovering it. Rather, I am endorsing Rorty's (1998) conclusion that the Platonic distinction between mere appearances and essential reality be abandoned entirely. This appearance/ reality distinction is a human invention (like every other belief or model for understanding the world) that has arguably outlived its usefulness (Rorty, 1999). Rather than continue to endorse the idea that beliefs should be divided between mere appearances and the real thing, or to give up on finding truth because the human condition makes it impossible to do so, I am suggesting that the helping professions would do better to abandon this distinction entirely. Upon hearing about my perspective, I am sometimes asked whether I think that there is a pure reality apart from human beliefs. My response is that I reject the dualistic assumption (between true reality and mere belief) inherent in the question. Answering the question would require me to accept a premise that I reject. Simply put, my pragmatist position is that beliefs should be judged according to the consequences of endorsing them. In other words, "the appearance reality distinction should be dropped in favor of a distinction between less useful and more useful ways of talking" (Rorty, 1998, p. 1).

However, if I were merely arguing that counselors should have good reasons for their interventions, the reader might reasonably charge that I have wasted far too much time exploring esoteric philosophical ideas to arrive at such an obvious conclusion. I am advocating for more than the simple idea that counselors should be able to provide justifications for their professional actions: I am trying to promote an attitudinal shift among helping professionals. By adopting an epistemological attitude that disavows the correspondence theory of truth, multiple benefits for individual helpers and the helping professions as a whole might be created, such as minimization of abuses of power in the counseling relationship, increased tolerance for human differences, and freedom from theoretical dogmatism. These practical payoffs are the primary reasons that counselors should abandon truth and base professional actions on reasonable, evolving justifications alone.

As a point of clarification, I am not advocating that counselors discuss these esoteric, philosophical ideas with clients. The last thing that suffering clients probably want to hear about is arid, academic issues that have no direct bearing on helping them to resolve their problems. However, counselors should carefully examine their own privately held philosophical assumptions because, as has been noted throughout this chapter, these assumptions often have subtle, but significant, consequences for the activity of professional helping.

Indeed, shifting from truth to justification as the criterion for judging interventions may not change much about the usual, overt practices of helping professionals. Using myself as an example, I was trained in a modernist, psychoanalytic paradigm and continue to use psychoanalytic conceptualizations and interventions to guide my professional practices. However, because I no longer consider psychoanalytic theory true in the modernist sense, I am now a more flexible practitioner whose full allegiance is to client betterment, not a theoretical orientation. Psychoanalytic conceptualizations and interventions often help clients; this is the only reason that I continue to use them. In the context of the helping encounter, then, the relative "truth" of a perspective should be judged according to whether the perspective promotes client betterment, not according to whether the perspective corresponds to the intrinsic nature of some reality. Beliefs can only reasonably be judged by the consequences of endorsing them.

In addition to clinical work, an attitudinal shift from truth to justification as the criterion for judging interventions can also provide benefits to other areas of the counseling profession. For instance, counseling supervisors sometimes have multiple supervisees, each of whom might have a different theoretical orientation, counseling style, and professional demeanor. If a supervisor subscribes to the idea that counseling should be guided by the intrinsic nature of the realities of the counseling situation, this attitude will severely limit the supervisor's ability to be respectful of and responsive to the multiple perspectives of the supervisees. Indeed, the supervisor might spend the supervisory time trying to indoctrinate supervisees into a particular system of thought. However, if the supervisor disavows the idea of truth, and, rather, helps supervisees determine whether their counseling interventions are justifiable, supervisees will still be subjected to an evaluative standard, but this standard will not yield the traditional side effects of truth claims, such as power plays, coercive indoctrination, intolerance of human differences, and the stifling of free, creative alternatives to traditional ideas and practices.

Professors in programs that train helping professionals, likewise, might gain similar benefits by adopting the attitude that the teaching enterprise should have nothing to do with modernist ideals of truth. Arguably, the atmosphere of the counseling classroom should provide an orientation to learning and growth that can serve as a model for students to adopt with their future clients. In this regard, education of helping professionals should promote critical thinking, the emergence of multiple perspectives, tolerance for ambiguity, and freedom to explore novel ideas. Truth is an intellectual straitjacket on these processes that, at worst, promotes indoctrination of students, places limits on discussions, and promotes intolerance of dissenting opinions. Judging ideas by an ever-evolving set of professional justifications, rather than by their correspondence to the intrinsic nature of reality, frees the class-room milieu from the damaging grip of truth.

Perhaps the reader might think that I have overstated the damage that can be caused by the overvaluation of truth. While I have admittedly presented a strong, at times dramatic, case against the correspondence theory of truth, I believe this type of presentation is necessary to raise consciousness about an epistemological value system that is usually hidden and unknown, even to those who hold it. Replacing discovered truth with ever-evolving justifications is arguably a vital attitudinal shift for professional helpers to make in order for the helping professions to advance to new levels of tolerance for diverse people, practices, and ideas.

Chapter Seven

The Journey Continues

I am incredibly grateful for my job as a professor. I was provided with a safe, secure position, outfitted with the resources necessary for intellectual adventures, and encouraged to vigorously pursue my curiosities, wherever they might take me. Indeed, they have taken me to some strange and interesting places. I visited new ideological lands where selves and realities melted before my eyes. I witnessed the frightening depths of the unconscious, glorious mountain tops of self-actualization, and vast, uncharted seas of psychological possibility. My travel diary has more questions than answers, but I have begun to connect the puzzle pieces I have collected along the way.

"What does it mean to know a client?" is a question that grew out of my lifelong sense of isolation. When I began my journey, I assumed that this question was obvious and self-evident. I no longer think that this is the case. Indeed, this question is simply a by-product of the Enlightenment philosophical tradition that idealizes isolated selves and willful individualism (Gergen, 1995, 1999; Rosenau, 1992). This tradition is neither foundational nor necessary. Philosophers constructed it centuries ago. Like all human constructions, the idea of isolated minds can simply be discarded when it no longer serves a useful purpose.

Without a philosophy of individualism, questions about knowing the interior of each other's minds become superfluous (Gergen, 1999; Rudes & Guterman, 2007). The question "What does it mean to know a client?" is merely fruit from an ideological tree that has no roots in any foundational soil. Alternatively, within a social constructionist position, which presumes that selves are fluid and continually reconstructed in social milieus (McNamee, 1996), questions about individual minds do not even arise. Questions are always by-products of assumptions. Assumptions are created by human beings. Discard the constructed assumptions, and the questions evaporate (Rorty, 1999).

An existentialist challenger might say that I have simply found an elaborate rationalization to avoid confronting one of the truisms of the human condition. "You are all alone," this challenger might say. "You can talk yourself out of death, too, but it is still coming for you." Perhaps (because I felt compelled to insert this existentialist challenger in the midst of my resolution) the reader can tell that I am still somewhat conflicted about human isolation. I suppose this is a good thing, though. A settled mind is a curse for an intellectual.

The psychoanalytic party lines that my professors taught me, my experiences with clients, the world beyond graduate school that placed little value on psychoanalysis, and my encounter with the empirical finding that all orientations work about equally well (Wampold, 2001) were a difficult set of experiences for me to reconcile. These experiences all seemed to boil down to one question: "What makes counseling effective?" Like my other questions, I do not claim to have found a definitive answer. However, the contextual model of treatment seems like a strong step in the right direction.

If healing is examined from a universalist, multicultural perspective, it becomes clear that the shaman, witch doctor, and counselor all do about the same thing (Frank & Frank, 2001; Torrey, 1972a). Each of these professionals is designated as a healer within their respective societies. These healers help sufferers combat demoralization by proffering healing narratives and associated rituals that members of the particular culture regard as curative, such as cognitive-behavioral interventions, the undoing of curses, or the restoration of one's soul. The experience of having a healing authority identify the causes of and cures for psychological distress instills hope, combats demoralization, and leads sufferers to a renewed sense of mastery over difficulties that formerly seemed insurmountable. As further evidence for this contextual model, I have observed that certain helping professionals (who vary widely in their favored treatment approaches) consistently obtain good results with their clients. From this observation, it is easy to conclude that it cannot be the treatment orientation that is responsible for client betterment. Indeed, Wampold (2001), whose comprehensive overview of decades of meta-analytic research strongly supported the contextual model, advised consumers of psychotherapy to seek a therapist who has a strong reputation for helping clients, regardless of theoretical orientation.

Endorsing the contextual model resolved some of my practical and theoretical questions, but it created additional philosophical problems. The contextual model trivializes the role of truth in healing. However, is this trivialization warranted? Should we presume that everything that counselors tell their clients is simply a by-product of cultural values about healing and never represents discovered truths? Or, can counselors discover objective truths about their clients? This line of inquiry was encapsulated in my third funda-mental question: Are truths discovered or created in the counseling relation-ship?

After she described her early family life to me, I asked a particular client whether it struck her as ironic that, in adulthood, she had recreated the hellish childhood that she had longed to escape. This client had apparently never considered the parallels between her early and contemporary lives. My re-mark had an enormous experiential impact on her, and she began to wonder whether a hidden part of herself had deliberately engineered her current state of suffering. In this case, my comment served as the impetus for deeper reflection and eventual lasting changes. Despite the obvious benefits of my intervention, a part of me could not help but wonder whether it was true. Did I discover a fact about my client, or did I simply create a clever and persua-sive (but untrue) perspective from the material that she had presented? Were the psychological benefits of my remark a sign that I had been correct, or was my client simply continuing to co-create this new, constructed narrative with me? These questions could conceivably be asked about every counseling intervention. In short, are truths discovered or created in the counseling rela-tionship?

My beginning answer to this third fundamental question is based on James' (1995) pragmatic method for testing questions: "What difference would it make to anyone if this notion rather than that notion were true? If no practical difference whatever can be traced, then the alternatives mean practi-cally the same thing, and all dispute is idle" (p. 18). Therefore, using James' pragmatic method, I think that it is probably of questionable value to pursue the discovery/creation question because the answer would make no practical difference about how to respond to a client. Counselors should respond in ways that are meaningful to clients, without regard for esoteric epistemolog-ical considerations. In this regard, I have argued that the dichotomy between discovery and creation in the counseling situation should be abandoned in favor of "emotional resonance" (Hansen, 2005b, p. 10). Counselors should not waste time philosophically fretting about whether their remarks are found or made (a distinction that makes no difference to practice) but focus their concerns on whether their interventions are experientially meaningful to cli-ents (a consideration that makes a difference).

Incidentally, James' (1995) pragmatic test has been an incredibly useful method for me to employ in my professional life. I try to use it frequently, particularly during meetings. Keep the following questions handy if, like me, you have little tolerance for lengthy meetings: "What practical difference would it make if we settled our current debate in one direction or the other? If it would make little or no practical difference, why should we waste our time discussing it?" After posing these questions, I have been able to quickly end meetings that probably would have lasted for hours.

Anyway, back to the four fundamental questions. My beginning answers to the second and third questions suggest a need for greater inquiry about the general role of truth in the helping professions. With regard to the second fundamental question, the factors that make counseling effective (i.e., contextual model) have nothing to do with truth. Likewise, the third question, which asks about the discovery of truth in counseling processes, can easily be dismissed as irrelevant. Because the construct of truth seems to be unimportant in key realms of counseling practice, this begs the larger, fourth fundamental question: Should counselors abandon the idea of truth?

Answering this question requires an extended foray into philosophy, much more so than the other three. Having delved into the philosophical literature, I have been persuaded that the correspondence theory of truth is logically indefensible (Rorty, 1999). In short, it makes no sense to sort beliefs and statements according to ones that match the intrinsic nature of reality (including client realities) and ones that do not. Not only is this truth-detecting practice unsupportable on logical grounds, the notion of discovered truth has caused horrendous abuses of power throughout human history generally (Foucault, 1984) and within the helping professions in particular (Masson, 1994). As a replacement for truth, I have offered the neopragmatic criterion that beliefs should be evaluated solely by the consequences of endorsing them, not by their supposed rootedness in the intrinsic nature of reality (Rorty, 1999).

As applied to counseling, interventions should be judged by the degree to which they bring beneficial consequences to clients, not according to whether, in the practitioner's judgment, they accurately correspond to the intrinsic nature of some client reality. Historically, fidelity to truth has caused helping professionals to be dogmatically tied to particular theoretical orientations instead of to client betterment. Truth has also been used to justify intolerance of marginalized groups and to engage in overt and subtle abuses of power in the therapeutic relationship. For these reasons, abandoning the correspondence theory of truth, in my opinion, would be a tremendous positive step forward for the helping professions.

It is important to note that I am not arguing that (a) objective truth does not exist; or (b) objective truth exists, but human beings are incapable of accessing it. Both of these statements are derived from a dualistic epistemological system, which presumes a dichotomy between truths and nontruths (i.e., mere appearances versus actual reality). Taking my cues from Rorty (1999), I am arguing that this dualistic epistemological system should be abandoned altogether. This dualistic system about knowing was constructed by philosophers thousands of years ago. Although it has been an important part of the Western intellectual tradition for millennia, it is merely a construction (like all beliefs and systems of thought) and can be abandoned when it no longer suits the purposes of human advancement. Without the epistemological dualisms of true versus not true, questions about whether someone has accessed the objective truth, or whether truth actually exists, become nonsensical. Instead of a dualistic epistemological system that divides human beliefs and statements into ones that are human distortions and others that are objectively true, I am advocating the adoption of a Darwinist system, which sorts beliefs and statements according to their adaptive utility. Within this system, the sole criterion for judging beliefs is the consequences of endorsing them. In short, "the appearance reality distinction should be dropped in favor of a distinction between less useful and more useful ways of talking" (Rorty, 1998, p. 1). Of course, I am not claiming that this neopragmatic epistemology is true in the correspondent sense. I am simply proposing a hopeful alternative to the modernist ideology that has served as the foundation for the helping professions over the past century.

These are my general, beginning answers to the four questions. I do not claim to have found the correct answers (whatever that would mean). Reasonable people could certainly disagree with every one of my conclusions. Indeed, I hope that my questions and answers generate dynamic debate, controversy, and continued dialogue, rather than static acceptance. Professions evolve by embracing conflicts, not by avoiding them. However, because my conclusions are the hard-won product of decades of research and reflection, and are a good fit for my intellectual disposition, I tend to value them. My investment in my conclusions raises an interesting fifth line of inquiry: Can the helping professions be structured around my conclusions? In what ways would the helping professions have to change to fully assimilate the intellectual products of my encounters with the four fundamental questions?

HOPES FOR THE FUTURE OF PROFESSIONAL HELPING

Over the past several decades, philosophical reflection, tolerance for ambiguity, and a focus on human meaning systems have been virtually eradicated from the helping professions (Hansen, 2009a). Rigidly defined diagnostic categories, treatment plans, and professional identities have supplanted the reflective and nuanced modes of thought that were formerly the professional norm. Whatever one thinks about this historical transformation, it has been a significant change in the basic ideological posture of the helping professions. It is interesting to speculate about the factors that have caused this massive ideological shift. This historical transformation has certainly not been due to cutting-edge research that has found that counselors should be more concrete, less reflective, and incorporate a greater amount of superficial, black-and-white style of thinking in their work. Indeed, this shift has taken place for at least three reasons, none of which have anything to do with client betterment. I am confident that two of these reasons (i.e., medicalization and the politics of professionalization) have undoubtedly been strong contributors to the current culture of professional helping. However, the third is somewhat speculative, but still worth considering.

Starting with the speculative reason, perhaps the move to a medicalized, diagnostic mental health culture has been a massive, group countertransference reaction on the part of the helping professions (Hansen, 2005a). Although forming intimate helping relationships can be very rewarding, practitioners can also become weary, anxious, frightened, envious, burned-out, resentful, vicariously traumatized, insecure, and psychologically unsettled when they continually maintain close empathic connections with their clients. Rather than suffer through chronic, recurring "onslaughts of client intimacy," (Hansen, 2005a, p. 412) perhaps, unconsciously, helping professionals have gradually incorporated and institutionalized ideological elements in their work that provide a psychological reprieve from the drain of continual empathic connection. A comfortable psychological distance is provided when clients are conceptualized as collections of symptoms (which is the ideological starting point of contemporary mental health culture) instead of as struggling individuals who might benefit from an intimate helping connection. In this regard, Shur (1994) proposed that the exorbitant paperwork and administrative requirements of modern inpatient psychiatric hospitals unconsciously serve to protect workers from close psychological contact with the terrifying subjective life of schizophrenics. Perhaps an analogous group countertransference reaction, unconsciously engineered to create psychological distance between helpers and clients, has occurred in mental health culture over the past three decades. Whatever one thinks of this speculative hypothesis, medicalization and the politics of professionalization have surely contributed to the current culture of helping.

The renewed rise of medicalization in contemporary mental health culture has its origins in the mid-1950s with the discovery of effective medications for severe mental health conditions (Shorter, 1997), research-based attacks on psychoanalytic outcomes (Eysenck, 1952), and the proliferation of new treatments, such as cognitive, behavioral, and humanistic approaches, which unseated psychoanalytic hegemony (Hansen, 2009a). However, during the 1980s, the combined influence of biological psychiatry (Shorter, 1997), the new DSM (Spiegel, 2005), the financial interests of pharmaceutical companies (Murray, 2009), and the rise of managed care (Hansen, 1997) jettisoned the medical model of mental health to a position of strong dominance in the helping professions. Regarding this dominance, I think that it is at least somewhat justifiable for the psychiatric profession to adopt the medical model. Psychiatric medications, while arguably wildly over prescribed, have indeed alleviated the mental suffering of numerous people. Therefore, a conceptual system that aligns particular disorders with pharmaceutical agents that have proven efficacy (i.e., medical model) is arguably a logical one for the psychiatric profession to adopt. To be clear, then, I am not taking a stance against the medical model (in and of itself) or the use of medications.

Remarkably, though, the nonprescribing helping professions have also adopted the medical model. Diagnostics, symptom-based treatment planning, and the prescription of specific techniques for particular disorders are now the norm in the talking therapies (Hansen, 2005a). Clearly, this trend toward medicalization has more to do with greed and professional status than with helping clients. Indeed, after an exhaustive review of outcome research, Wampold (2001) concluded that specific techniques (the use of which are promoted by the medical model) account for less than 1 percent of the variance in treatment outcomes. This finding should not come as a surprise to anyone, given that the quality of the therapeutic relationship is the within-treatment factor that has consistently been shown to be most highly associated with outcomes (Lambert, 1992; Wampold, 2001). Indeed, all one has to do is reflect on his or her own relationships to conclude that the application of techniques usually does nothing to promote intimate relating. If, after telling me that she had a difficult day, I responded to my wife by recommending a technical intervention to help her with the problem that she is having with her mood, this would certainly not be a relationship-enhancing moment. There is no reason to believe that the guidelines for intimate relationship formation should be different depending on whether the parties are positioned inside or outside of a counseling office. The medical model, then, because it promotes the use of specific techniques for particular conditions, is clearly of very limited use for nonprescribing professionals, whose healing power is derived from the quality of the counseling relationship.

As a pragmatist, however, I am not arguing that the medical model (or any other model) is inherently good or bad. Conceptual models are tools. As such, arguing about the worth of the medical model is akin to arguing about the worth of particle accelerators; they are good for physicists, but useless for violinists. It is impossible to determine the value of any tool, including ideological tools, without connecting the tool to a use. The medical model may be a good idea for helping professionals with pills, but it is generally a bad idea for those without them.

In addition to medicalization, the politics of professionalism have strongly contributed to the demise of a focus on human meaning systems within the helping professions (Hansen, 2010c). By "politics of professionalization," I am referring to the efforts by professional organizations to gain increases in status, power, and money. These efforts, which are aimed at advancing helping professions in the public sphere, often have deleterious ideological consequences for the educators and practitioners who operate within the professions. Although my doctorate is in clinical psychology, my professional allegiance shifted to the counseling profession shortly after I graduated and was hired as a professor in a department of counseling. Therefore, many of my specific examples about professionalization are drawn from the counseling profession, although the general principles I cite are applicable to all helping professions.

When I first became a part of the counseling profession during the early 1990s, I was attracted to the free and open nature of the profession. There were active debates, a diverse pool of ideas, and an attitude of acceptance about various intellectual stances. Many of these qualities still exist, which is one of the reasons that my professional experience as a counselor educator has been so satisfying. However, over the years, the politics of professionalization have begun to erode and restrict the ideological freedoms that I cherish.

For instance, according to the body that currently accredits counseling programs (i.e., Council for Accreditation of Counseling & Related Educational Programs), professional outsiders (like myself because my doctorate is in clinical psychology) can only be hired under certain, restrictive conditions. If I had graduated during the past few years, and had applied to counseling departments for a faculty position, I would never have been hired because of this new regulation. Notably, other helping professions have had this restrictive disciplinary rule in place, either formally or informally, long before it was implemented by the counseling profession.

As another (somewhat ironic) example of the suppression of diversity by professional politics, the counseling profession has strongly aligned itself with the multicultural and social justice movements. Related helping professions have made similar ideological commitments to the value of diversity. Multiculturalism and social justice are completely reasonable and laudable trends, of course. Appreciating human diversity and championing the oppressed are important values for helping professionals to adopt. However, as these movements have become institutionalized, they have dictated and restricted modes of professional thought by defining competencies, regulating the types of scholarship that are acceptable, and creating rules for the inclusion of certain topics in counseling curricula (Hansen, 2008, 2010c). It is ironic that these movements, which were founded on the value of diversity, have resulted in restrictive regulations that have discouraged free and open intellectual activity. As institutions, then, the multicultural and social justice movements have spread the disease that they were originally designed to cure.

These politics and restrictions on professional freedom are perhaps most blatantly represented by the movement to define the professional identity of counselors. Other helping professions have engaged in analogous politically motivated efforts to define themselves. However, these efforts have been a particularly prominent part of the politics of professional counseling recently, probably because mental health counseling came onto the professional scene decades after social work and psychology had already arrived. There-fore, it is understandable that counselors have felt a strong urgency to carve out a unique identity for themselves that distinguishes them from their long established competitors.

Despite the professional advancement that identity definitions can some-times bring, people involved in professional identity movements should con-sider Foucault's insights about identity:

> There are two meanings of the word *subject*: subject to someone else by control and dependence, and tied to his own identity by a conscience or self-knowledge. Both meanings suggest a form of power which subjugates and makes subject to (Foucault, 1983, p. 212).

In other words, identity definitions are subjugating, disempowering, and re-strictive. The more something is defined, the less free it is to be something else. By honing in on a particular definition of counselor identity, profession-al identity advocates are automatically restricting alternative identity pos-sibilities.

Although I have critiqued the politics that have placed restrictions on intellectual freedom within counseling and related helping professions, I understand that these same politics can be useful at the legislative level. Counseling lobbyists need to be armed with quick, handy responses to legis-lators and influential politicians who might reasonably ask "who are counse-lors? and "what do they do?" Without tidy, pre-packaged responses, it would be impossible for the profession to make any political headway, advance its influence, or secure power. I respect my colleagues who engage in these political efforts, and I have certainly benefited from their hard work.

However, problems ensue when the methods and tools used for profes-sional advancement in the political realm are generalized to other profession-al areas. It is harmful and damaging to professional progress for the simple, singular, and concrete formulations that advance the profession at the politi-cal top to be pushed down to and disseminated throughout the rest of the profession. Practitioners, who are continually confronted with a vast array of human differences, should embrace a decentered, relativistic epistemology that endorses the legitimacy of multiple world views and flexible self-definitions (Polkinghorne, 1992). Furthermore, the creative work of re-searchers and theoreticians should not be encumbered by restrictive profes-sional formulations, which are designed for an entirely different purpose. Using simple, concrete ideologies for the purposes of education, practice, and scholarship is analogous to using paint-by-number kits to advance the work of professional artists.

Simply put, different tools should be used for different purposes. The types of tools used to promote the helping professions at the political level are grossly incompatible with the types of tools needed to advance the helping professions in other realms. Problems ensue when the ideological tools connected with power and money (e.g., medical model, identity definitions, etc.) are adopted by all areas of the helping professions. A separatist approach (i.e., using different ideologies for different purposes), instead of trying to unify all professional life under a single ideological banner, would keep simplistic and concrete ideological tools from suppressing the focus on human meaning systems, which has traditionally and rightfully been the hallmark of relational helping. Indeed, I would go so far as to say that it may be an ideological conflict of interest for professors to engage in the politics of professional advancement, because the narrow, restrictive, definitions that this advancement requires are completely counter to the goals of academia, which are to challenge, enrich, complicate, and decenter traditional ideas to achieve new perspectives and greater levels of understanding. As a further step to retain a focus on human meaning systems, I have also suggested that counseling should be structured by the values of the humanities rather than the by values of science (Hansen, 2012a).

In this regard, my humanities colleagues in history, English, and philosophy departments study human meaning systems. Progress in their disciplines consists of complicating the subject of study and offering new perspectives. These humanities professionals may use science as a tool to support their work (e.g., carbon dating of artifacts for archaeologists and historians). However, the overarching spirit of their professions is defined by the study of human meaning systems. In contrast, my colleagues in biology, chemistry, and physics attempt to hone in on singular explanations and systematically eliminate extraneous points of view. The nuances of human meaning are generally not important to these scientists, who, instead, seek to discover singular answers to the puzzles of nature that are of concern to them. Neither emphasis (i.e., complicating subject matter with human meaning systems or narrowing down findings with science) is inherently better than the other. Representatives from different academic disciplines have simply adopted the foundational ideology that best facilitates advances in their scholarly realm.

Counselors and psychotherapists make their living by immersing themselves in the complexities of human meaning systems. Professional helping necessarily involves a deep appreciation for, and continual effort to understand, the ways that clients make sense out of their experiences. Therefore, I have argued that the professional life of counselors should be structured by the values of the humanities, not the values of science (Hansen, 2012a). Active debate, qualitative research, and an appreciation for the multiple layers of meaning that are present in any human interaction should be the norm for counselors. Certainly, science is a vital tool for the helping professions to retain, particularly as it is used to generate outcome research. However, the scientific values of parsimony and the goal of discovering singular truth should not be allowed to overtake the helping professions, which make progress by cultivating complexity and creating new possibilities for human transformation.

DISCUSSION

Philosophical discussions can be interesting and illuminating, but almost none of the practitioners whom I admire care much about esoteric intellectual issues; they are too busy helping their clients to be concerned with such matters. These practitioners are the real heroes of the profession, not professors like me, who practice part-time and then scurry back to the safety of academia and the realm of ideas. I hope that this book has provided some of these practitioners with an intellectual respite from the difficult, draining, and noble work that they do.

With regard to philosophical issues, the best counselors know that counseling is simply an extended conversation between two people that relies on authenticity, trust, and gut-wrenching emotional honesty; cerebral formulations or flashy techniques have little to do with it. With this in mind, I would like to remind the reader about the reflective task that I cited in a previous chapter. Specifically, I often instruct my supervisees and students to engage in a simple exercise to disabuse them of the notion that counseling is a highly technical process. I ask my trainees to recall a time when they felt troubled, talked to someone about what was bothering them, and left the conversation feeling hopeful, renewed, and unburdened. I deliberately instruct them not to tell me about the nature of their problem, but only to report what the person who helped them said or did. The result of this experiment is almost always the same. Trainees consistently report that the helper listened intently, showed signs of empathy, struggled to understand the problem from the trainee's point of view, and refrained from judgment. "If this is what helped you," I say, "why would you think that your clients would need something highly technical or radically different?"

In this regard, people have probably sought relief from their suffering by talking to others since humans acquired the ability to speak. There is nothing new or particularly innovative, then, about the modern counseling scenario, wherein one person helps the other through conversational means. Indeed, with some rare exceptions, if you were to observe virtually any individual counseling session that has occurred over the past century, all you would see is two people talking (Hansen, in press).

The seeming simplicity of this helping scenario is in stark contrast to the complex labyrinth of professionalized mental health culture with its licensure regulations, educational standards, ethical codes, supervisory mandates, accreditations, and continuing education requirements. There is no shortage of complicating factors within academia, too. Bizarre research agendas, arbitrary programmatic requirements, arcane theorizing, irrelevant coursework, and esoteric vocabularies, which often obscure far more than they illuminate, are all parts of the standard, generally unquestioned, educational process that prospective professional helpers are required to endure.

In terms of these simplicity versus complexity polarities, I have spent the better part of my career complicating professional helping by raising and examining philosophical issues. This strange way of making a living has certainly been enjoyable and has helped me to provide for my family. Every time that I have been in the grips of some new conceptual puzzle, though, I have always asked myself, "is this level of complexity really warranted?" Regardless of the answer to this question, the ability to simultaneously describe counseling as a simple, intuitive process, on the one hand, and as a highly complex encounter worthy of continual scholarly scrutiny, on the other, has always had a strong, hypnotic appeal to me. There is something engagingly aesthetic, intellectually addictive, and mesmerizingly elegant about the juxtaposition of commonsensical simplicity and high technical complexity within the same subject matter.

Although philosophical questioning adds complexity to the helping paradigm, I believe that it can also serve a revelatory function, cutting through the static of the complexity and revealing the basic foundations of what counseling should be. This book has been devoted to philosophical questioning. I certainly hope that it has served to illuminate more than unnecessarily complicate. As a proposed extension of this intellectual enterprise, my strategy for answering questions throughout much of my career has been to import philosophical ideas into professional helping to enrich and critique understandings of counseling processes. In turn, I think that philosophy, as a discipline, could probably benefit from assimilating insights from psychotherapy and counseling. Dry, philosophical theorems take on new meaning and life when they are positioned within the intersubjective matrix of the helping encounter.

Notably, though, effective practitioners do not grandiosely presume that they possess complex, esoteric truths about the human condition that their unfortunate clients were somehow unable to acquire, but approach their work with a sense of humility, awe, and openness to ever changing perspectives. These values are summarized by Rorty's (1989) concept of the liberal ironist, which I believe is a good ideal for practitioners and scholars alike to adopt. Ironists humbly recognize that their conclusions are never grounded in the intrinsic nature of reality, thereby always making their conclusions subject to revision. Liberals, according to the definition adopted by Rorty, are people who believe that "cruelty is the worst thing we do" (p. 85). Do not be cruel, and always be willing to change your perspective if presented with good reasons for doing so. I cannot think of a better ideal for helping professionals than the liberal ironist.

As this book draws to a close, I am reminded that much of the emotional impetus that fueled my philosophical explorations (and perhaps my entire professional life) was a longstanding sense of isolation. However, I now realize that the inevitability of existential isolation is merely a conclusion drawn from a particular intellectual tradition, which can easily be discarded for a more hopeful perspective. Indeed, to take a social constructionist stance, neither you, dear reader, nor I have been alone. By reading this book you have created your own meanings in response to the words that I have put on these pages. In this respect, you have been an author as much as a reader. Indeed, together we have created a unique, timeless space of meaning that can never be recreated or undone. This space represents an ongoing bond, which is a sure sign that we do not have to be alone.

References

American Psychiatric Association (2000). *Diagnostic and statistical manual of mental disorders.* (4th ed., text revision). Washington, D.C.: Author.

Anderson, W. (1990). *Reality isn't what it used to be: Theatrical politics, read-to-wear religion, global myths, primitive chic, and other wonders of the postmodern world.* San Francisco, CA: Harper & Row.

Arlow, J., & Brenner, C. (1964). *Psychoanalytic concepts and the structural theory.* New York: International Universities Press.

Ary, D., Jacobs, L. C., & Sorensen, C. (2010) *Introduction to research in education* (8th ed.). Belmont, CA: Wadsworth.

Baudrillard, J. (1995). The map precedes the territory. In W. Anderson (Ed.), *The truth about the truth: De-confusing and re-constructing the postmodern world* (pp. 79–81). New York, NY: G. P. Putnam's Sons.

Beck, A. (1976). *Cognitive therapy and the emotional disorders.* New York, NY: International Universities Press.

Berg, B. (2004). *Qualitative research methods for the social sciences* (5th ed.). Boston, MA: Allyn & Bacon.

Berne, E. (1961). *Transactional analysis in psychotherapy: A systematic individual and social psychiatry.* New York, NY: Grove Press.

Beutler, L. E., & Clarkin, J. (1990). *Differential treatment selection: Toward targeted therapeutic interventions.* New York, NY: Brunner/Mazel.

Bohart, A. (1990). A cognitive client-centered perspective on borderline personality development. In G. Lietaer, J. Rombauts, & R. Van Balen (Eds.), *Client-centered and experiential psychotherapy in the nineties* (pp. 599–621). Leuven, Belgium: Leuven University Press.

Brenner, C. (1973). *An elementary textbook of psychoanalysis.* New York, NY: International Universities Press.

Budd, R., and Hughes, I. (2009). The dodo bird verdict—Controversial, inevitable and important: A commentary on 30 years of meta-analyses. *Clinical Psychology and Psychotherapy, 16*, 510–22.

Camus, A. (1955). *The myth of Sisyphus and other essays.* New York, NY: Knopf.

Chessick, R. D. (1996). The application of postmodern thought to the clinical practice of psychoanalytic psychotherapy. *Journal of the American Academy of Psychoanalysis, 24*, 385–407.

Chodoff, P. (2002). The medicalization of the human condition. *Psychiatric Services, 53*, 627–628.

Custance, A., & Travis, L. (1980). *The mysterious matter of mind.* Grand Rapids, MI: Zondervan.

140   References

Davidson, L. (2000). Philosophical foundations of humanistic psychology, *Humanistic Psychologist, 28,* 7–31.

DeCarvalho, R. (1990). A history of the "third force" in psychology. *Journal of Humanistic Psychology, 30,* 22-44. doi:10.1177/002216789003000403

Dennett, D. (1995). *Darwin's dangerous idea: Evolution and the meanings of life.* New York, NY: Simon & Schuster.

Derrida, J. (1995). The play of substitution. In W. Anderson (Ed.), *The truth about the truth: De-confusing and re-constructing the postmodern world* (pp. 86-95). New York, NY: G.P. Putnam's Sons.

Descartes, R. (1988). *Descartes: Selected philosophical writings.* New York: Cambridge University Press.

deShazer, S. (1985). *Keys to solution in brief therapy.* New York: W.W. Norton.

Eagle, M. (2011). *From classical to contemporary psychoanalysis: A critique and integration.* New York, NY: Routledge.

Elkins, D. (2009). *Humanistic psychology: A clinical manifesto; a critique of clinical psychology and the need for progressive alternatives.* Colorado Springs, CO: University of the Rockies Press.

Ellis, A., & Grieger, R. (1977). *Handbook of rational-emotive therapy.* New York, NY: Springer.

Eysenck, H. J. (1952). The effects of psychotherapy: An evaluation. *Journal of Consulting Psychology, 16,* 319–24.

Eysenck, H., & Wilson, G. (1973). *The experimental study of Freudian theories.* London: Methuen.

Fancher, R. (1995). *Cultures of healing: Correcting the image of American mental health care.* New York, NY: Freeman.

Festinger, L. (1957). *A theory of cognitive dissonance.* Stanford, CA: Stanford University Press.

Flax, J. (1990). *Thinking fragments: Psychoanalysis, feminism, & postmodernism in the contemporary west.* Berkeley, CA: University of California Press.

Foucault, M. (1965). *Madness and civilization; a history of insanity in the age of reason.* New York, NY: Pantheon.

———. (1980). C. Gordon (Ed.), *Power/Knowledge; selected interviews and other writings 1972–1977* (C. Gordon, L. Marshall, J. Mepham, & K. Soper, Trans.). New York, NY: Pantheon.

———. (1983). The subject and power. In H. Dreyfus & P. Rabinow, *Michel Foucault: Beyond structuralism and hermeneutics* (2nd ed.). (pp. 208–226). Chicago, IL: University of Chicago Press.

———. (1984). P. Rabinow (Ed.), *The Foucault reader.* New York, NY: Pantheon.

Fowers, B., & Richardson, F. (1996). Individualism, family ideology and family therapy. *Theory and Psychology, 6,* 121–51.

Frances, A. (2009). Whither DSM-V? *British Journal of Psychiatry, 195,* 391–92. doi: 101192/bjp.bp.109.073932

Frank, J. D., & Frank, J. B. (1991). *Persuasion and healing* (3rd ed.). Baltimore, MD: Johns Hopkins University Press.

Frederickson, J. (1999). *Psychodynamic psychotherapy: Learning to listen from multiple perspectives.* Philadelphia, PA: Brunner/Mazel.

Freud, S. (1953). Freud, S. (1953). The interpretation of dreams. In J. Strachey (ed. & trans.), *The standard edition of the complete psychological works of Sigmund Freud* (Vols. 4 & 5). London: Hogarth Press. (Original work published 1900).

———. (1955). Analysis of a phobia in a five-year-old boy. In J. Strachey (Ed. and Trans.), *The standard edition of the complete psychological works of Sigmund Freud* (Vol. 10, pp. 3-149). London: Hogarth Press. (Original work published 1909).

———. (1957). The future prospects of psycho-analytic therapy. In J. Strachey (Ed. and Trans.), *The standard edition of the complete psychological works of Sigmund Freud* (Vol. 11, pp. 139-151). London: Hogarth Press. (Original work published 1910).

————. (1958a). Recommendations to physicians practicing psycho-analysis. In J. Strachey (Ed. and Trans.), *The standard edition of the complete psychological works of Sigmund Freud* (Vol. 12, pp. 109-120). London: Hogarth Press. (Original work published 1912).

————. (1958b). The dynamics of transference. In J. Strachey (Ed. and Trans.), *The standard edition of the complete psychological works of Sigmund Freud* (Vol. 12, pp. 97-108). (Original work published 1912)

————. (1959). The question of lay analysis. In J. Strachey (Ed. and Trans.), *The standard edition of the complete psychological works of Sigmund Freud* (Vol. 20, pp. 183-258). London: Hogarth Press. (Original work published 1926).

————. (1961a). Civilization and its discontents. In J. Strachey (Ed. and Trans.), *The standard edition of the complete psychological works of Sigmund Freud* (Vol. 21, 57-145). London: Hogarth Press. (Original work published 1930)

————. (1961b). The ego and the id. In J. Strachey (Ed. and Trans.), *The standard edition of the complete psychological works of Sigmund Freud* (Vol. 19, pp. 12-66). (Original work published 1923)

————. (1963). Introductory lectures on psycho-analysis. In J. Strachey (Ed. & Trans.), *The standard edition of the complete psychological works of Sigmund Freud* (Vols. 15 & 16). London: Hogarth Press. (Original work published 1916)

Gabbard, G. (2005) *Psychodynamic psychiatry in clinical practice* (4th ed.). Arlington, VA: American Psychiatric Publishing.

————. (2010). *Long-term psychodynamic psychotherapy: A basic text.* (2nd ed.). Washington, D.C.: American Psychiatric Publishing.

Gabbard, G., Litowitz, B., & Williams, P. (2012). *Textbook of psychoanalysis* (2nd ed.). Arlington, VA: American Psychiatric Publishing.

Gay, P. (1988). *Freud: A life for our time.* New York, NY: W.W. Norton.

Gergen, K. (1991). *The saturated self: Dilemmas of identity in contemporary life.* New York, NY: Basic Books.

————. (1995). The healthy, happy human being wears many masks. In W. Anderson (Ed.), *The truth about the truth: De-confusing and re-constructing the postmodern world,* (pp. 136–50). New York: G.P. Putnam's Sons.

————. (1999). *An invitation to social construction.* Thousand Oaks, CA: Sage.

Gill, M. (1994). *Psychoanalysis in transition: A personal view.* Hillsdale, NJ: Analytic Press.

Gladding, S., & Yonce, C. (1986). A bridge between psychoanalysis and humanistic psychology: The work of Heinz Kohut. *Journal of Counseling and Development, 64,* 536–37.

Glover, E. (1931). The therapeutic effect of inexact interpretation. *International Journal of Psycho-Analysis, 12,* 397–411.

Grosskurth, P. (1987). *Melanie Klein: Her world and her work.* Cambridge, MA: Harvard University Press.

Guindon, M., Green, A., & Hanna, F. (2003). Intolerance and psychopathology: Toward a general diagnosis for racism, sexism, and homophobia. *American Journal of Orthopsychiatry, 73,* 167–76.

Halling, S., & Nill, J. D. (1995). A brief history of existential-phenomenological psychiatry and psychotherapy. *Journal of Phenomenological Psychology, 26,* 1–45.

Hansen, J. T. (1997). The impact of managed care on the therapeutic identity of psychotherapists. *Psychotherapy in Private Practice, 16,* 53–65. doi:10.1300/J294v16n03_04.

————. (2000). Psychoanalysis and humanism: A review and critical examination of integrationist efforts with some proposed resolutions. *Journal of Counseling & Development, 78,* 21–28. doi: 10.1002/j.1556-6676.2000.tb02556.x.

————. (2002). Postmodern implications for theoretical integration of counseling orientations. *Journal of Counseling & Development, 80,* 315–21. doi: 10.1002/j.1556-6678.2002.tb00196.x.

————. (2003). Including diagnostic training in counseling curricula: Implications for professional identity development. *Counselor Education and Supervision, 43,* 96–107. doi: 10.1002/j.1556-6978.2003.tb01834.x.

————. (2004). Thoughts on knowing: Epistemic implications of counseling practice. *Journal of Counseling & Development, 82,* 131–38. doi: 10.1002/j.1556-6678.2004.tb00294.x.

———. (2005a). The devaluation of inner subjective experiences by the counseling profession: A plea to reclaim the essence of the profession. *Journal of Counseling & Development, 83,* 406–15. doi: 10.1002/j.1556-6678.2005.tb00362.x.

———. (2005b). Postmodernism and humanism: A proposed integration of perspectives that value human meaning systems. *Journal of Humanistic Counseling, Education and Development, 44,* 3–15. doi: 10.1002/j.2164-490X.2005.tb00052.x.

———. (2005c). Truth or consequences: A neopragmatic critique of contemporary mental health culture. *Journal of Mental Health Counseling, 27,* 210–20.

———. (2006a). Counseling theories within a postmodernist epistemology: New roles for theories in counseling practice. *Journal of Counseling & Development, 84,* 291–97. doi: 10.1002/j.1556-6678.2006.tb00408.x.

———. (2006b). Discovery and creation within the counseling process: Reflections on the timeless nature of the helping encounter. *Journal of Mental Health Counseling, 28,* 289–308.

———. (2006c). Humanism as moral imperative: Comments on the role of knowing in the helping encounter. *Journal of Humanistic Counseling, Education and Development, 45,* 115–25. doi: 10.1002/j.2161-1939.2006.tb00011.x.

———. (2006d). Is the best practices movement consistent with the values of the counseling profession? A critical analysis of best practices ideology.*Counseling and Values, 50,* 154–60. doi: 10.1002/j.2161-007X.2006.tb00051.x.

———. (2007a). Counseling without truth: Toward a neopragmatic foundation for counseling practice. *Journal of Counseling & Development, 85,* 423–30. doi: 10.1002/j.1556-6678.2007.tb00610.x.

———. (2007b). Epistemic contradictions in counseling theories: Implications for the structure of human experience and counseling practice. *Counseling and Values, 51,* 111–24. doi: 10.1002/j.2161-007X.2007.tb00069.x.

———. (2007c). Relational and transcendental humanism: Exploring the consequences of a thoroughly pragmatic humanism. *Journal of Humanistic Counseling, Education and Development, 46,* 131–41. doi: 10.1002/j.2161-1939.2007.tb00031.x.

———. (2007d). Should counseling be considered a health care profession? Critical thoughts on the transition to a health care ideology. *Journal of Counseling & Development, 85,* 286–93. doi: 10.1002/j.1556-6678.2007.tb00476.x.

———. (2008). Copying and coping conceptualizations of language: Counseling and the ethic of appreciation for human differences. *International Journal for the Advancement of Counselling, 30,* 249–61. doi:10.1007/s10447-008-9061-1.

———. (2009a). On displaced humanists: Counselor education and the meaning-reduction pendulum. *Journal of Humanistic Counseling, Education and Development, 48,* 65–76. doi: 10.1002/j.2161-1939.2009.tb00068.x.

———. (2009b). Self-awareness revisited: Reconsidering a core value of the counseling profession. *Journal of Counseling & Development, 87,* 186–93. doi: 10.1002/j.1556-6678.2009.tb00566.x.

———. (2010a). Consequences of the postmodernist vision: Diversity as the guiding value for the counseling profession. *Journal of Counseling & Development, 88,* 101–07. doi: 10.1002/j.1556-6678.2010.tb00156.x.

———. (2010b). Ideas on the margins: Professional counseling and ideological insularity. *International Journal for the Advancement of Counselling, 32,* 214–24. doi: 10.1007/s10447-010-9102-4.

———. (2010c). Multiplicity and its discontents: Life on the counseling farm. *International Journal for the Advancement of Counselling, 32,* 240–47. doi: 10.1007/s10447-010-9103-3.

———. (2012a). Extending the humanistic vision: Toward a humanities' foundation for the counseling profession. *Journal of Humanistic Counseling, 51,* 133–44. doi: 10.1002/j.2161-1939.2012.00011.x.

———. (2012b). The future of humanism: Cultivating the humanities' impulse in contemporary mental health culture. *Self & Society: An International Journal of Humanistic Psychology, 40,* 21–5.

————., (in press). Talking about counseling: A plea to return to humanistic language. *Journal of Humanistic Counseling.*

Hicks, S. (2004). *Explaining postmodernism: Skepticism and socialism from Rousseau to Foucault.* Milwaukee, WI: Scholargy Publishing.

Hoffman, I. (1998). *Ritual and spontaneity in the psychoanalytic process: A dialectical-constructivist view.* Hillsdale, NJ: Analytic Press.

Jacoby, R. (1983). *The repression of psychoanalysis: Otto Fenichel and the political Freudians.* Chicago, IL: University of Chicago Press.

James, W. (1995). *Pragmatism.* New York, NY: Dover Publications.

Janov, A. (1970). *The primal scream; Primal therapy: The cure for neurosis.* New York, NY: Putnam.

Jones, M. (1953). *The therapeutic community.* New York, NY: Basic Books.

Kahn, E. (1985). Heinz Kohut and Carl Rogers: A timely comparison. *American Psychologist, 40,* 893–904.

Kant, I. (2007). *Critique of pure reason.* London, England: Penguin.

Kaslow, F. (1993). Relational diagnosis: Past, present and future. *American Journal of Family Therapy, 3,* 195–204.

Kirk, S., & Kutchins, H. (1994). The myth of reliability of DSM. *Journal of Mind and Behavior, 15,* 71–86.

King, R. (1986). Self-realization and solidarity: Rorty and the judging self. In J. H. Smith & W. Kerrigan (Eds.), *Pragmatism's Freud: The moral disposition of psychoanalysis,* (pp. 28–51) Baltimore, MD: Johns Hopkins University Press.

Kirschenbaum, H. (2007). *The life and work of Carl Rogers.* Ross-On-Wye, UK: PCCS Books.

Kirsner, D. (2000). *Unfree associations: Inside psychoanalytic institutes.* London: Process Press.

Kohut, H. (1971). *The analysis of the self.* New York, NY: International Universities Press.

Kottler, J. (2010). *On being a therapist* (4th ed.). San Francisco, CA: Jossey-Bass.

Kuhn, T. (1996). *The structure of scientific revolutions* (3rd ed.). Chicago, IL: University of Chicago Press.

Lambert, M. J. (1992). Psychotherapy outcome research: Implications for integrative and eclectic therapists. In J. C. Norcross & M. R. Goldfried (Eds.), *Handbook of psychotherapy integration* (pp. 91–129). New York, NY: Basic Books.

Lazarus, A. A. (1981). *The practice of multimodal therapy.* New York, NY: McGraw-Hill.

Leibert, T. (2012). Response to Hansen: Economic pressures, not science, undermine humanistic counseling. *Journal of Humanistic Counseling, 51,* 206–16.

Loftus, E., and Ketcham, K. (1994). *The myth of repressed memory: False memories and allegations of sexual abuse.* New York, NY: St. Martin's Griffin.

————. (1994). *The myth of repressed memory: False memories and allegations of sexual abuse.* New York: Saint Martin's Press.

Loftus, E., & Pickrell, J. (1995). The formation of false memories. *Psychiatric Annals, 25,* 720–25.

Lordes, A. (1984). *Sister outsider: essays and speeches.* Freedom, CA: Crossing Press.

Lyotard, J. F. (1984). *The post-modern condition: A report on knowledge.* Minneapolis, MN: University of Minnesota Press.

Mahoney, M. (1991). *Human change processes: The scientific foundations of psychotherapy.* New York, NY: Basic Books.

Makari, G. (2008). *Revolution in mind: The creation of psychoanalysis.* New York, NY: HarperCollins.

Marquis, A., & Douthit, K. (2006). The hegemony of "empirically supported treatment": Validating or violating? *Constructivism in the Human Sciences, 11,* 108–41.

Maslow, A. (1968). *Toward a psychology of being* (2nd ed.). New York, NY: Van Nostrand Reinhold.

Masson, J. M. (1984). *The assault on truth: Freud's suppression of the seduction theory.* New York, NY: Farrar, Straus, & Giroux.

Masson, J. M. (1994). *Against therapy.* Monroe, ME: Common Courage Press.

Matson, F. (1971). Humanistic theory: The third revolution in psychology. *Humanist, 12,* 7–11.

Mayes, R., & Horwitz, A.V. (2005). DSM-III and the revolution in the classification of mental illness. *Journal of the History of the Behavioral Sciences, 41,* 249–67. doi: 10.1002/jhbx.20103.

McNamee, S. (1996). Psychotherapy as a social construction. In H. Rosen & K. Kuchlwein (Eds.), *Constructing realities: Meaning-making perspectives for psychotherapists* (pp. 115–137). San Francisco, CA: Josey-Bass.

McWilliams, N. (1999). *Psychoanalytic case formulation.* New York, NY: Guilford.

———. (2004). *Psychoanalytic psychotherapy: A practitioner's guide.* New York, NY: Guilford.

———. (2005). Preserving our humanity as therapists. *Psychotherapy: Research, Practice, Training, 42,* 139–51.

———. (2011). *Psychoanalytic diagnosis: Understanding personality structure in the clinical process* (2nd ed.). New York, NY: Guilford Press.

Menand, L. (2001). *The metaphysical club: A story of ideas in America.* New York, NY: Farrar, Straus, & Giroux.

Messer, S., & Wampold, B. (2002). Let's face facts: Common factors are more potent than specific therapy ingredients. *Clinical Psychology: Science and Practice, 9,* 21–25.

Messer, S., & Warren, C. (1995). *Models of brief psychodynamic therapy: A comparative approach.* New York, NY: Guilford.

———. (2001). Understanding and treating the postmodern self. In J. Muran (Ed.), *Self-relations in the psychotherapy process,* (pp. 193–209). Washington, D.C.: American Psychological Association.

Minuchin, S. (1974). *Families and family therapy.* Cambridge, MA: Harvard University Press.

Morris, J. (1994). The history of managed care and its impact on psychodynamic treatment. *Psychoanalysis and Psychotherapy,* 11, 129–37.

Moss, D. (2001). The roots and genealogy of humanistic psychology. In K. Schneider, J. Bugental, & J. F. Pierson (Eds.), *The handbook of humanistic psychology: Leading edges in theory, research, and practice* (pp. 5–20). Thousand Oaks, CA: Sage.

Muran, J. (2001). An introduction: Contemporary constructions and contexts. In J. Muran (Ed.), *Self-relations in the psychotherapy process,* (pp. 3–44) Washington, D.C.: American Psychological Association.

Murray, T. (2009). The loss of client agency into the psychopharmaceutical-industrial complex. *Journal of Mental Health Counseling, 31,* 283–308.

Myers, J.E., & Sweeney, T.J. (2005). *Counseling for wellness: Theory, research, and practice.* Alexandria, VA: American Counseling Association.

Orange, D. (2011). *The suffering stranger: Hermeneutics for everyday clinical practice.* New York, NY: Taylor & Francis.

Orange, D. M. (1995). Emotional understanding: Studies in psychoanalytic epistemology. New York, NY: Guilford Press.

Parker, I. (2007). *Revolution in psychology: Alienation to emancipation.* Ann Arbor, MI: Pluto Press.

Perls, F. (1969). *Gestalt therapy verbatim.* Lafayette, CA: Real People Press.

Pine, F. (1990). *Drive, ego, object, and self; a synthesis for clinical work.* New York, NY: Basic.

Plato. (1968). *The republic of Plato* (A. Bloom, Trans.). New York, NY: Basic Books.

Pollak, R. (1997). *The creation of Dr. B: A Biography of Bruno Bettelheim.* New York, NY: Touchstone.

Polkinghorne, D. (1992). Postmodern epistemology of practice. In S. Kvale (Ed.), *Psychology and postmodernism* (pp. 146–65). Thousand Oaks, CA: Sage.

Reiss, B. (2008). *Theaters of madness: Insane asylums & nineteenth-century American culture.* Chicago, IL: University of Chicago Press.

Rogers, C. (1957). The necessary and sufficient conditions of therapeutic personality change. *Journal of Consulting Psychology, 21,* 95–103.

———. (1986). Reflection of feelings. *Person-Centered Review* 1, 375–77.

Rorty, R. (1979). *Philosophy and the mirror of nature.* Princeton, NJ: Princeton University Press.

———. (1982). *Consequences of pragmatism.* Minneapolis, MN: University of Minnesota Press.

———. (1986). Freud and moral reflection. In J. H. Smith & W. Kerrigan (Eds.), *Pragmatism's Freud: The moral disposition of psychoanalysis* (pp. 1–27). Baltimore, MD: Johns Hopkins University Press.

———. (1989). *Contingency, irony, and solidarity.* New York, NY: Cambridge University Press.

———. (1991). *Objectivity, relativism, and truth.* New York, NY: Cambridge University Press.

———. (1998). *Truth and progress; philosophical papers, volume 3.* New York: Cambridge University Press.

———. (1999). *Philosophy and social hope.* New York, NY: Penguin Putnam.

———. (2000a). Response to Robert Brandom. In R. Brandom (Ed.), *Rorty and his critics* (pp. 183–90). Malden, MA: Blackwell.

———. (2000b). Universality and truth. In R. Brandom (Ed.), *Rorty and his critics* (pp. 1–30). Malden, MA: Blackwell.

Rosenau, P. (1992). *Post-modernism and the social sciences: Insights, inroads, and intrusions.* Princeton, NJ: Princeton University Press.

Rudes, J., & Guterman, J. (2007). The value of social constructionism for the counseling profession: A reply to Hansen. *Journal of Counseling & Development, 85,* 387–92.

Sass, L. (1989). Humanism, hermeneutics, and humanistic psychoanalysis: Differing conceptions of subjectivity. *Psychoanalysis and Contemporary Thought, 12,* 433–504.

Schmitt, F. (1995). *Truth: A primer.* Boulder, CO: Westview Press.

Seligman, M. (1995). The effectiveness of psychotherapy: The *Consumer Reports* study. *American Psychologist, 12,* 965–974.

Shaler, J. (Ed.). (2004). *Szasz under fire: The psychiatric abolitionist faces his critics.* Chicago, IL: Open Court.

Shapiro, F. (1995). *Eye movement desensitization and reprocessing (EMDR): Basic principles, protocols, and procedures.* New York, NY: Guilford.

Shorter, E. (1997). *A history of psychiatry; from the era of the asylum to the age of prozac.* New York, NY: Wiley & Sons.

Shur, R. (1994). *Countertransference enactment: How institutions and therapists actualize primitive internal worlds.* Northvale, NJ: Aronson.

Skinner, B. (1974). *About behaviorism.* New York, NY: Knopf.

Smith, M. L., & Glass, G. V. (1977). Meta-analysis of psychotherapy outcome studies. *American Psychologist, 32,* 752–60.

Spence, D. (1982). *Narrative truth and historical truth: Meaning and interpretation in psychoanalysis.* New York, NY: W.W. Norton & Company.

Spiegel, A. (January 3, 2005). The dictionary of disorder: How one man revolutionized psychiatry. *New Yorker,* 56–63.

Sterba, R. (1982). *Reminiscences of a Viennese psychoanalyst.* Detroit, MI: Wayne State University Press.

Stolorow, R., Atwood, G., & Orange, D. (2002). *Worlds of experience: Interweaving philosophical and clinical dimensions in psychoanalysis.* New York, NY: Basic Books.

Stolorow, R., Brandchaft, B, & Atwood, G. (1995). *Psychoanalytic treatment: An intersubjective approach.* Hillsdale, NJ: Analytic Press.

Storr, A. (1989). *Freud: A very short introduction.* New York, NY: Oxford University Press.

Strenger, C. (1991). *Between hermeneutics and science: An essay on the epistemology of psychoanalysis.* Madison, CT: International Universities Press.

Sugarman, A. (1977a). Object-relations theory: A reconciliation of phenomenology and ego psychology. *Bulletin of the Menninger Clinic, 41,* 113–30.

———. (1977b). Psychoanalysis as a humanistic psychology. *Psychotherapy: Theory, Research, and Practice, 14,* 204–11.

Szasz, T. (1961). *The myth of mental illness.* New York, NY: Harper.

————. (1970). *The manufacture of madness: A comparative study of the Inquisition and the mental health movement.* New York, NY: Harper & Row.

————. (1977). *Psychiatric slavery.* New York, NY: Free Press.

————. (1994). Cruel compassion: Psychiatric control of society's unwanted. New York, NY: Wiley.

————. (2007a). *Coercion as cure: A critical history of psychiatry.* New Brunswick, NJ: Transaction Publishers.

————. (2007b). *The medicalization of everyday life.* Syracuse, NY: Syracuse University Press.

————. (2008). *Psychiatry: The science of lies.* Syracuse, NY: Syracuse University Press.

Tarnas, R. (1991). *The passion of the Western mind: Understanding the ideas that have shaped our world view.* New York, NY: Harmony.

Tobin, S. (1990). Self psychology as a bridge between existential-humanistic psychology and psychoanalysis. *Journal of Humanistic Psychology, 30,* 14–63.

Torrey, E. (1972a). *The mind game: Witchdoctors and psychiatrists.* New York, NY: Emerson Hall.

————. (1972b). What Western psychotherapists can learn from witchdoctors. *American Journal of Orthopsychiatry, 42,* 69–76.

Truax, C.B., & Carkhuff, R.R. (1967). *Toward effective counseling and psychotherapy.* Chicago, IL: Aldine.

Ventola, C. L. (2011). Direct-to-consumer pharmaceutical advertising: Therapeutic or toxic? *Pharmacy and Therapeutics, 36,* 669–84.

Wachtel, P. (1977). Psychoanalysis and behavior therapy: Toward an integration. New York, NY: Basic Books.

Wampold, B. (2001). *The great psychotherapy debate: Models, methods, and findings.* Mahwah, NJ: Erlbaum.

Watson, J. (1919). *Psychology from the standpoint of a behaviorist.* Philadelphia, PA: Lippincott. doi:10.1037/10016-000.

Whitaker, R. (2002). *Mad in America: Bad science, bad medicine, and the enduring mistreatment of the mentally ill.* Cambridge, MA: Perseus.

————. (2010). *Anatomy of an epidemic: Magic bullets, psychiatric drugs, and the astonishing rise of mental illness in America.* New York: NY: Broadway Paperbacks.

White, M., & Epston, D. (1990). *Narrative means to therapeutic ends.* New York, NY: W.W. Norton.

Whitehead, A. N. (1979). *Process and reality: An essay in cosmology.* New York, NY: Free Press.

Wolpe, J. (1958). *Psychotherapy by reciprocal inhibition.* Stanford, CA: Stanford University Press.

Yalom, I. (1980). *Existential psychotherapy.* New York, NY: Basic Books.

————. (1989). *Love's executioner and other tales of psychotherapy.* New York, NY: Basic Books.

Index

About the Author

James T. Hansen is a professor at Oakland University in the Department of Counseling. Dr. Hansen has published about fifty refereed articles in leading counseling journals. He is also the coeditor of an award-winning book on humanism. Dr. Hansen has over twenty-five years of experience as a practitioner, supervisor, and consultant.

CPSIA information can be obtained at www.ICGtesting.com
Printed in the USA
BVOW08*2005151113

336247BV00002B/6/P